T0311670

# Seven Democratic Virtues of Liberal Education

This book argues that the liberal arts and sciences (LAS) model of education can inspire reform across higher education to help students acquire crucial civic virtues.

Based on interviews with 59 students from LAS programmes across Europe, the book posits that LAS education can develop a range of citizenship skills that are central to the democratic process. The interviews provide insight into how studying LAS prepares students for citizenship by asking them to reflect on their education, what it taught them, and how it did so. Building on these insights, seven key democratic competencies are identified and linked to concrete educational practices that foster them, leading to an agenda for higher education reform.

Ultimately arguing for making the teaching of civic virtue a more central part of university education in Europe, this book will appeal to researchers, educators, and politicians with an interest in education policy, philosophy of education, and democratic theory, as well as concerned citizens.

**Teun J. Dekker** is Professor of Liberal Arts and Sciences Education, University College Maastricht – Maastricht University, The Netherlands.

# Routledge Research in Character and Virtue Education

This series provides a forum for established and emerging scholars to discuss the latest debates, research and theory relating to virtue education, character education and value education.

# Seven Democratic Virtues of Liberal Education

A Student-Inspired Agenda for Teaching Civic Virtue in European Universities

**Teun J. Dekker**

Routledge
Taylor & Francis Group
LONDON AND NEW YORK

First published 2023
by Routledge
4 Park Square, Milton Park, Abingdon, Oxon OX14 4RN

and by Routledge
605 Third Avenue, New York 10158

*Routledge is an imprint of the Taylor & Francis Group, an informa business*

© 2023 Teun J. Dekker

*British Library Cataloguing-in-Publication Data*
A catalogue record for this book is available from the British Library

*Library of Congress Cataloging-in-Publication Data*
Names: Dekker, Teun, 1980- author.
Title: Seven democratic virtues of liberal education : a student-inspired agenda for teaching civic virtue in European universities / Teun J. Dekker.
Description: Abingdon, Oxon ; New York, NY : Routledge, 2023. | Series: Routledge research in character and virtue education | Includes bibliographical references and index.
Identifiers: LCCN 2022038853 (print) | LCCN 2022038854 (ebook) | ISBN 9781032369211 (hardback) | ISBN 9781032369228 (paperback) | ISBN 9781003336594 (ebook)
Subjects: LCSH: Education, Humanistic—Europe. | Civics, European—Study and teaching (Higher) | Education, Higher—Political aspects—Europe. | Citizenship—Europe. | Democracy and education—Europe.
Classification: LCC LC1024.E85 D45 2023 (print) | LCC LC1024.E85 (ebook) | DDC 370.11/2094—dc23/eng/20220926
LC record available at https://lccn.loc.gov/2022038853
LC ebook record available at https://lccn.loc.gov/2022038854

ISBN: 978-1-032-36921-1 (hbk)
ISBN: 978-1-032-36922-8 (pbk)
ISBN: 978-1-003-33659-4 (ebk)

DOI: 10.4324/9781003336594

Typeset in Times New Roman
by Apex CoVantage, LLC

*This book is dedicated to Hans Adriaansens, for simply doing it and having faith that students would make it work.*

# Contents

# Note to the Reader

The data that support the findings of this book are available on request from the author. The data are not publicly available as they contain information that could compromise the privacy of research participants. The metadata are registered at: https://doi.org/10.34894/ZWKS0Y

# About the Author

Teun J. Dekker is Professor of Liberal Arts and Sciences Education at University College Maastricht – Maastricht University, in The Netherlands. He is an evangelist for liberal education in Europe and seeks to promote this philosophy through research, teaching, institutional innovation, and consulting on policy.

# Preface

This book grew out of my inaugural lecture as Professor of Liberal Arts and Sciences Education at University College Maastricht – Maastricht University. Inaugural lectures are, by their very nature, self-congratulatory affairs, and there is always a risk that they turn into public relations exercises, particularly if they are given by self-professed evangelists. I am aware that, as someone who has spent his career arguing in favour of liberal arts and sciences education, I can hardly be considered an independent, dispassionate observer. At the same time, if professors of liberal arts and sciences education cannot be for liberal education, then who can? They may do a better or worse job in their use of evidence and methodology, and they should be judged on that basis. However, they should not be blamed for having the courage of their convictions. Hence, this book argues unabashedly that liberal education can help future generations develop the skills that they will need to be good citizens in democratic societies. Since democracy itself is a normative ideal, it does not seem inappropriate for contributions to debates about democratic education also to take a stand. As such, my efforts should ultimately be judged on whether they convince others to change their views and excite them into reconsidering what university education should be. After all, as an educator, inspiration is my core business.

However, inspiration rarely comes out of nowhere, and I have many debts to acknowledge. I owe much to the three books that have been my guiding stars throughout this project: Martha Nussbaum's *Cultivating Humanity: A Classical Defense of Reform in Liberal Education*,[1] teaching me about liberal education; Robert Dahl's *Democracy and Its Critics*,[2] teaching me about democracy; and William Perry's *Forms of Intellectual and Ethical Development in the College Years: A Scheme*,[3] teaching me how to listen to students. Gwyn Williams provided sterling editing, helping me see my own mistakes. But most importantly, I am very grateful to the liberal arts and sciences programmes that hosted me and to the future citizens who shared their understandings of what this whole liberal arts and sciences thing is about and why it matters. This book springs from a concern for democracy as a way of living together. While there are many reasons to fear for its future, the young people I spoke to make me hopeful that, as we like to say at University College Maastricht, everything will be OK.

## Notes

1 Martha Nussbaum, *Cultivating Humanity: A Classical Defense of Reform in Liberal Education* (Cambridge, MA: Harvard University Press, 1998).
2 Robert Dahl, *Democracy and Its Critics* (New Haven, CT: Yale University Press, 1989).
3 William Perry, *Forms of Intellectual and Ethical Development in the College Years: A Scheme* (New York: Holt, Rinehart, and Winston, 1970).

## References

Dahl, Robert. *Democracy and Its Critics*. New Haven, CT: Yale University Press, 1989.

Nussbaum, Martha. *Cultivating Humanity: A Classical Defense of Reform in Liberal Education*. Cambridge, MA: Harvard University Press, 1998.

Perry, William. *Forms of Intellectual and Ethical Development in the College Years: A Scheme*. New York: Holt, Rinehart, and Winston, 1970.

# 1 A Renewed Call for Civic Education in Universities

Aristotle famously concluded *Politics*, his treatise on the organisation of the state, with a discussion of education. He understood that if people are to live together successfully, the attitudes and skills they bring to their interactions are more important than formal institutions. Certainly, the structure of society frames those interactions, but no system of government can work unless citizens make it work by behaving in accordance with the principles of that system. This means that the long-term success of any political community depends on teaching future generations the civic virtues of that community. Education, which has the goal of preparing young people for their futures, has a large role to play in this socialisation process. That makes education a political institution. As Aristotle put it:

> That which contributes most to preserving the state is, what is now most despised, to educate your children for the state; for the most useful laws, and most approved by every statesman, will be of no use if the citizens are not accustomed to and brought up in the principles of the political system.[1]

However obvious that truth may have been to Aristotle, much of contemporary European higher education seems to have forgotten that it, too, must contribute to the cultivation of civic virtue. Universities in Europe, and indeed elsewhere, mainly see themselves as teaching academic skills and preparing students to participate in the economy. They rarely understand their mission as helping students to become better citizens. This is a missed opportunity; higher education is a powerful but underused tool to help future generations acquire the skills and dispositions they will need to participate in the political system. Given the many challenges European democracies face, it is imperative that universities do their bit to ensure the next generation of citizens is able to meet those challenges. This, however, will require a significant paradigm shift in thinking about the purposes and methods of higher education.

DOI: 10.4324/9781003336594-1

Historically, higher education was very much concerned with the cultiva-tion of civic virtue. In ancient Greece and Rome, one of the major goals of education was to help free people, i.e., those who were not slaves, develop the skills they needed to participate in public life. This liberal tradition of education carried on through medieval times and into the modern age, giv-ing rise to what we know now as liberal arts and sciences (LAS) education.[2] This educational philosophy is prominent in the United States, although even there the civic aspect of liberal education is increasingly questioned, and more emphasis is placed on employability.

In Europe, however, higher education has moved away from the liberal tradition over the last few centuries. German institutions, as well as higher education systems influenced by the Germanic tradition, came to emphasise research-based education in specific academic disciplines, while French institutions saw themselves as preparing students for roles in state bureau-cracies. It is only in the past 30 years or so that European innovators in higher education have created new LAS programmes. These programmes are diverse in setup and function in very different contexts, but they consti-tute something of an educational model that differs sharply from that which predominates in higher education on the continent. This liberal model has great potential to inspire European higher education to better teach the civic virtues students require to participate in democracy. Reviving the liberal tradition of higher education is our best bet for reinvigorating the teaching of civic virtue in Europe and thereby enabling our democracies to live up to their highest aspirations.

## The Liberal Education Model in Europe

Drawing on the LAS tradition from North America and responding to cur-rent developments in thinking about multidisciplinarity[3] and student-cen-tred education, liberal education, as it has emerged in Europe over the past 30 years, has several roots. On the one hand, a range of programmes was set up in Central and Eastern Europe after the fall of communism. During authoritarian times, universities had the role of reproducing party elites and propagating the official ideology. When the communist regimes ended, it was essential to consider how higher education could be reformed to suit newly free societies. While most institutions chose to follow the typical European model, a group of educators felt that the moment demanded a more ambitious reform agenda. Under the moniker of *Artes Liberales*, they gathered several times to discuss the future of higher education in Central and Eastern Europe and initiated LAS programmes that operate to this day.[4]

A number of Western European countries began to establish their own LAS programmes a few years later, albeit for different reasons. Around the time of the Bologna Agreement of 1999, which initiated a far-reaching harmonisation of higher education in Europe based on the Bachelor's/ Master's model of a three-year undergraduate first cycle and a one- or two-year graduate cycle, Dutch sociologist Hans Adriaansens started the first so-called University College in the Netherlands. Adriaansens believed that Dutch higher education was not in good shape, with its high drop-out rates, mono-disciplinary programmes, and anonymous pedagogies. The LAS programme he established represented a radical departure from the mainstream of Dutch higher education. He aimed to set an example of how higher education could be organised differently, and, in rapid succession, several Dutch universities started their own University Colleges. The success of the LAS movement in the Netherlands did not go unnoticed, with universities in the United Kingdom (which were also inspired by the US) and, to a lesser extent, Germany starting similar programmes.[5] As more LAS programmes were created, variations started to emerge. Some programmes had a thematic curriculum, focusing, for example, on global challenges, while others were more integrated with their host universities or functioned as satellite campuses.

There are now over 80 programmes in Europe that self-identify as offering liberal education, with numbers continuing to grow.[6] Still, one should not overestimate the success of the LAS movement, as these programmes currently enrol less than 1% of students in Europe and the exponential growth of recent years has subsided. At the same time, one can speak of a genuine, pan-European movement; not only do LAS programmes share an educational model, but they also work together in a range of overlapping national and international networks.

Liberal education programmes depart considerably from the classical model of higher education in Europe. Traditionally, much of European higher education has been organised around mono-disciplinary programmes, such as law, economics, or medicine, which are primarily aimed at preparing students for professional careers. They typically employ conservative pedagogies, such as large-scale lectures and closed-book exams that require students to simply regurgitate what they have learned. They are also fairly transactional in how they relate to students, seeing teaching as a formal process of following courses, doing assessments, and receiving credits for those assessments until all requirements are met and a degree is issued. Although in other ways European higher education is highly diverse – all kinds of different institutions exist, catering to different populations, with different resource levels, different pedagogical and curricular profiles, and different educational cultures – this picture rings true for much of higher education across the continent.[7] Of course, one should not draw a caricature of European university education either; there are many programmes and institutions that have already departed from the traditional model, for example by offering more multidisciplinary curricula or small-scale pedagogies. This is a welcome change, one to which this book aims to contribute. However, this development is very much in progress, and there is still much work to be done to make such approaches to higher education the standard in Europe.

While there is a large variety of LAS programmes, they share several features that set them apart from the traditional model. They differ in terms of curriculum, pedagogy, and educational setting. Firstly, LAS programmes offer students a much more diverse curriculum, combining a general education in a range of subjects that are deemed valuable in their own right with more specialised study in a range of related disciplines. This ensures that LAS students acquire a multidisciplinary understanding of the issues they study. Students often have considerable freedom to choose which courses to take and to combine different disciplines, and they are typically supported in this by academic advisors or personal tutors. Moreover, programmes stress holistic development and the cultivation of generic intellectual skills, such as writing, argumentation, presentation, and research methodology, over narrow professional preparation. They are not intended to educate students for specific careers, leaving specialisation to the Master's phase or the workplace.

Secondly, LAS programmes offer active student-centred pedagogies. Rather than large lectures, in which professors present information to students in a monologue, occasionally interrupted by questions, these programmes use small-scale tutorials and seminars, and they ask students to take a much more active and engaged role in their education. This can take many forms, but the key is that students are given the opportunity to take the lead in discussing the material and to find their own perspectives on the issues they are studying. There must be opportunities for direct teacher-student interaction but also for student-to-student teaching. This active approach carries through to how LAS programmes assess their students. They typically de-emphasise traditional, proctored exams that focus on the reproduction of facts in favour of essays, assignments, presentations, and the like, in which students are asked to apply knowledge and research methods to issues they are interested in. Often these projects are group assignments in which students must work together to produce a larger piece of academic work.

Thirdly, LAS programmes emphasise the importance of educational relationships and create an academic community of learners who not only study together but also engage outside of the classroom in a social and extra-curricular context, sometimes even living together on a residential campus. The goal is to ensure a high level of social density and to make sure that students do not feel that they are anonymous passers-by going through a teaching factory. Rather, LAS programmes aim to be places where everybody knows your name and where students develop themselves not only intellectually, but also emotionally and socially. Many such programmes actively recruit students internationally, seeking to ensure that their communities are diverse places. Some offer scholarships to enable students from a wide range of socio-economic backgrounds to attend.

## Listening to Students

To understand how studying in a LAS programme helps students develop the civic virtues they will need to become good citizens, an obvious first step is to ask them how they experience their education. Hence, the main basis for the argument that LAS education can help students cultivate civic virtue is a significant number of interviews conducted with students in LAS programmes across Europe. In these interviews, students reflected on their education, what it taught them, and how it did so. These interviews present the lived experiences of students, offering greater insight into how liberal education prepares them for democratic citizenship better than the traditional quantitative methods. Civic virtues are, by their very nature, subtle, complex, and largely dispositional. As such, they are not easy to measure, and there is no reliable scale of citizenship ability. Even if it were possible to accurately assess how well citizens are prepared for doing their democratic duty, it would still be impossible to determine what contribution their education made to the development of the relevant skills, as one could never control for other factors. Nor could one identify the mechanisms at work, which would be required to implement reform in other contexts. Listening to students who are actually studying in LAS programmes, however, promises to provide a rich understanding of how their experiences affect them, which allows for an in-depth consideration of the democratic potential of liberal education.

Some might argue that asking students to reflect on their education is of limited use. For one thing, students have little to no experience with the democratic process, so they are unable to assess how their education prepares them for that process. Also, LAS programmes make all kinds of claims in brochures, during open days, and on websites about the education they offer and how it is supposed to benefit students, but these claims are largely rhetorical and have not been subject to much scientific scrutiny. Students might internalise these claims and come to understand their education in those terms. Or LAS programmes might simply attract students who are predisposed to developing certain democratic competencies because of their interests or socio-economic backgrounds.

Despite these objections, the voices of students are worth listening to. They are the ones who live their education on a daily basis. Indeed, they are the only ones who see all facets of the programmes they attend. They will have made a conscious choice to study LAS, even though this is not an obvious path in Europe, and they will have had many occasions to reflect on their education. Moreover, their observations, concerns, and remarks are evocative and insightful. Perhaps the interviews do not tell the full story about the democratic potential of liberal education, but they are certainly a part of that story. As always, the proof of the pudding is in the eating. The evidence presented here may or may not convince the reader, but it seems obvious that if one wants to understand how liberal education shapes students, one should, at the very least, include their perspectives.

To that end, 59 students from 14 LAS programmes in five European countries were interviewed, following a protocol that was approved by an ethical review committee.[8] The students attended Amsterdam University College, Bard College Berlin, Bratislava International School of Liberal Arts, Liberal Arts at King's College London, Liberal Arts and Sciences at Utrecht University, Liberal Arts and Sciences at Warsaw University, Leiden University College, Studium Individuale at Leuphana University, University College Freiburg, University College Groningen, Arts and Sciences at University College London, University College Maastricht, University College Tilburg,[9] and University College Utrecht. Since LAS education is most prominent in the Netherlands, it is appropriate to focus the sample on this country. The additional programmes represent the other main areas where LAS is a feature of the education landscape. The programmes differ in several respects. Some focus on global challenges, while others are built around the interaction between arts and sciences. A number of programmes are residential, but others do not offer their students accommodation. Some programmes are small, independent colleges, while others are embedded within major research universities. Some are highly selective while others are not. As a result, the sample gives a fairly broad picture of LAS education in Europe. In most cases, the interviews took place on campus, but the students from Berlin, Bratislava, and Warsaw were interviewed during a conference; as a result, the number of students interviewed from these programmes was somewhat lower than from the other programmes.

To ensure that they had significant experience with studying liberal arts, students were typically in their second or final year of the programme. They were recruited by programme coordinators, either through personal connections or through mailing lists. As such, it is likely that the students who participated in the study were particularly reflective about their education because they either volunteered to be interviewed or had previously interacted with the coordinators of their programmes. Hence, this is not a random sample, but rather a sort of convenience sample. It does not include a control group of students in traditional programmes to compare the experiences of the two groups. It is difficult to judge the extent to which the students interviewed are representative of the entire populations in their LAS programmes. However, their answers do display a great deal of convergence, and towards the end of the interview process, data-saturation was observed, meaning that little to no new information was found in the last interviews. During the interviews, students also made many generalised statements about their programmes, explaining how they thought the typical student experienced their education. Even if selection bias ensured that only students who were particularly engaged with their education were interviewed, the interviews still show what LAS education can do for students, and this is something of a basis for demonstrating the democratic potential of this educational model.

One or two days before their interviews, students were sent an informed consent form and digital questionnaire. The goal of this questionnaire was to get students to reflect on the main themes the semi-structured interview would discuss so that their answers would be more considered. The survey had questions about the point of LAS education, why freedom of choice in the curriculum was valuable, how students discussed their education with others, how LAS students should approach their studies, common criticisms of LAS education, the value of LAS education for students' economic and civic futures, and a final question on how studying LAS had changed them as people. For each question, students were asked to indicate their agreement with a series of statements on a 1 to 10 scale, with 1 representing complete disagreement and 10 representing complete agreement. It is important to note that the questionnaire was merely a starting point for the conversations. The scores served no purpose other than to identify topics of conversation and they have little meaning in isolation. They are included below for reference's sake but do not play a major role in the following chapters.

The questionnaire touched explicitly on the relationship between LAS education and democracy in two places. Firstly, in the opening question, in which students were asked to reflect on what LAS education meant to them, one statement read: *To me, liberal arts and sciences education is about becoming a good citizen in a democratic society.* On average, students awarded this item a score of 6.4 out of 10, behind their agreement with statements such as *To me, liberal arts and sciences education is about combining multiple academic disciplines in an in-depth way* (7.7), and *To me, liberal arts and sciences education is about developing myself broadly by gaining basic familiarity with a wide range of academic disciplines* (8.0), but ahead of *To me, liberal arts and sciences education is about learning about great research or famous books* (5.4). Secondly, and most significantly, democracy featured in a section in which there were two questions about the civic aspects of LAS education. This section was introduced as follows:

> Liberal arts and sciences programmes sometimes present themselves as not only educating future workers but also future citizens in democratic societies. Here are some questions about how you think about the relationship between liberal arts and sciences and democratic citizenship.

One question explored how students conceived of good citizenship, asking how important various behaviours and activities are in a democracy. The list of options was based on a common-sense understanding of various forms of political activity in a democracy. The question read as follows, with the average scores indicated in parentheses:

> As a citizen in a democratic society, I think it is important to
> . . . vote in elections (8.1)
> . . . know about the law, the political process, and the institutions of government (7.4)
> . . . stay informed about current events (7.8)
> . . . get in touch with political leaders (4.3)
> . . . be a member of a political party (2.9)
> . . . participate in direct political action, such as demonstrations (5.8)
> . . . run for a political position (2.8)
> . . . donate money to political causes (3.1)
> . . . volunteer for an NGO (4.9)

The other question considered how studying LAS had taught students certain things that one might think are important for citizenship. The list of statements was based on a rudimentary conception of the theory of civic virtue that will be presented in Chapter 2. The question read:

> Studying Liberal arts and sciences has made me
> . . . inclined to participate in the democratic process in some way (6.2)
> . . . able to understand the perspectives of other people (7.9)
> . . . able to think about the consequences of social choices for different groups of people (7.8)
> . . . able to explain my own position and circumstances to others, and to present my perspective and reasoning on certain topics to the wider community (7.6)
> . . . weigh perspectives and arguments, to come to reasoned conclusions about what should be done (7.9)
> . . . make and accept compromises (6.9)

During the actual interviews, conducted by the researcher in a secluded setting, students' responses to the questionnaire were discussed in detail. Interviews typically lasted slightly less than an hour. Students were asked to elaborate on scores that seemed interesting, either because they were different from other scores that the student gave or were particularly high or low. They tended to justify their choices but also sometimes reconsidered their scores. This often led to follow-up questions, links with previous answers, and enticing digressions. These were pursued enthusiastically, as it was within these further discussions that students could express themselves most freely.

The conversations were transcribed by a specialised company and pseudonymised before being analysed using qualitative data-analysis software. This software allows exchanges relating to particular topics to be coded as such and grouped together for further analysis. Fragments of different conversations that relate to the same issue can be linked, revealing common themes and shared understandings. The process of coding is part art and part science. It cannot be done algorithmically but requires complex interpretative judgements. To a certain extent, it is a matter of creative assembly, and, as in all creative processes, the hand of the creator is never completely invisible. One must piece together a large number of different elements and pursue trails of ideas to construct a coherent story about the democratic potential of LAS education. In doing this, one must navigate between two coding strategies. On the one hand, there is inductive coding, in which one simply seeks to systematise what one finds in the interviews, without preconceptions or prior theoretical assumptions. In this way, thematic codes emerge. On the other hand, there is deductive coding, in which one has a pre-existing set of categories and seeks to fit the data into them, to confirm or illustrate one's theory.

In this case, a hybrid approach was chosen. Only coding inductively might have presented an interesting picture of how students perceive their education, but not necessarily contributed to understanding how they develop the civic virtues that are key to the democratic process. The concept of democracy and the civic virtues that support it are independent of how students perceive them. They are ultimately justified by philosophical reflection on fundamental democratic values. Of course, one may ask whether students recognise the importance of certain virtues, as the first question on the civic potential of LAS education in the questionnaire did. This helps reveal how they see their role as future citizens. But students believing something to be a democratic virtue does not make it so. Hence, some pre-existing theory is required. At the same time, a purely deductive analysis, in which the seven virtues are already fully defined, would not have done justice to the distinctive contribution liberal education can make to democratic citizenship, as it would not have been open to the particularities of students' experiences and what they learn in their education.

The questionnaire, interviews, and analysis took a rough and ready conception of the democratic process and the virtues associated with it as a structuring device. In particular, the question on the democratic potential of LAS education contained a number of potential virtues. Similarly, during the analysis, a basic theoretical understanding of democracy served as a basis for identifying relevant exchanges and the kinds of categories that needed to be created. However, the particular definition of the virtues that this book presents, as well as the book's argument about how LAS education contributes to their development, were filled in based on the data. In other words, keeping in mind a general conception of what democracy is and how citizens should participate in it, the data were examined for content that related to that general conception, which in turn was broken down into separate virtues based on what was found. By going back and forth between theory and data, a conception of the democratic virtues of liberal education was defined that has two properties. On the one hand, this conception reflects the experiences of students, so that one can be somewhat confident that liberal education indeed teaches these virtues. On the other hand, the virtues the book presents also relate to a theoretically plausible conception of democracy, so that these virtues do, in fact, support the functioning of this system of government.

Concretely, the first step consisted of identifying all exchanges in the transcripts that related to democracy and what is required to be a good citizen. In total, 393 such exchanges were found. Keeping in mind the conception of democracy defined in the next chapter, these exchanges were then analysed again to find clusters of similar ideas that were thematically grouped and labelled, resulting in the seven virtues. From there, the rest of the discourse was examined for exchanges that related to these virtues with the aim of exploring which aspects of LAS education contribute to their development. The evidence that is presented in each chapter is drawn from these groupings of data. The chapters ask how the virtue should be understood, why it is indeed a democratic virtue, and how particular features of the LAS model contribute to its development. All quotes were lightly edited for grammar and clarity, but always with a concern for preserving their tone and intent.

## Seven Democratic Virtues

To make the case that liberal education helps students develop certain civic virtues and that this can inspire reform of the higher education system, Chapter 2 will consider the nature of civic virtue in a democracy. It will explore the nature of the concept and its role in political systems and show how a decline in civic virtue explains many of the challenges contemporary democracy faces. Building on this understanding of the importance of civic virtue, the chapter will then specify, with more precision than is commonly done, what sorts of skills, knowledge, and attitudes citizens must possess to optimally participate in the democratic process. Central to the argument is the idea of a democratic conversation, a special kind of exchange between citizens that models the essential values of democracy. Good citizens are those who can participate in such a conversation, and the civic virtues required for democracy are those that enable this participation. Reflecting on the nature of this special kind of conversation leads to the identification of the seven virtues that will be discussed, by showing how they facilitate and sustain democratic conversations.

This raises the question of how citizens are to acquire these virtues. Chapter 3 will argue that education, especially higher education, is a key venue for cultivating civic virtue. This follows from a basic understanding of the function of education in society that is supported by a long philosophical tradition. There are, of course, many counterarguments to the claim that higher education should cultivate civic virtue. Some might argue that only a limited fraction of the population attends university and hence teaching civic virtue in higher education violates the democratic norm of equality, or that the fundamental mandate of universities is academic and that politicising them comes at the expense of their scientific mission. These are indeed important concerns, and they will be considered but ultimately rejected.

The next seven chapters explore the democratic virtues of liberal education in greater detail, explaining exactly what each is and why it is important for democratic citizenship, before considering how liberal education, as practised in Europe, contributes to students developing it. Needless to say, the seven virtues are hardly the only things that students learn in a LAS programme. They also acquire scientific and theoretical knowledge, as well as a range of skills that will prepare them for graduate education and the labour market. Furthermore, they develop themselves personally and socially. As such, LAS education has many other, non-civic virtues. Nor are the seven virtues the only virtues that might be beneficial for citizenship in a democracy. One might be a good member of a democratic society in many ways, and such a society needs people who bring different competencies and dispositions to the governing process. Nevertheless, these chapters aim to show that the seven virtues are indeed democratic virtues, and that liberal education is a way of cultivating them.

Firstly, liberal education helps students develop *open-mindedness*, which should be understood as the realisation that one does not have all the answers at the outset, that one's preconceptions can be wrong, and that there might be good reasons to change one's mind on any number of matters. While several features of the LAS model can contribute to this realisation, it is perhaps most closely linked to the multidisciplinary nature of the typical LAS curriculum. Secondly, LAS teaches *independence of thought*, the ability to question received wisdom and to scrutinise the positions of others, to judge what is valuable in them and what is to be discarded. This is most closely associated with the active, student-centred pedagogies LAS programmes employ. Thirdly, LAS education gives students a *sense of self*, a developed conception of their identities, their self-interest, and their views on the problems society faces. Freedom to design one's own curriculum and freedom in assignments are features of LAS programmes that contribute to this. Fourthly, liberal education gives students a *sense of the other*, an understanding of other people's perspectives, interests, and circumstances, in part by having a highly international and diverse student body. Fifthly, group work and shared assignments teach students the art of *compromise*. Sixthly, LAS programmes promote *knowledge of social issues*, an awareness of the significant common problems and challenges society faces, in part by insisting that students take general education courses. Lastly, liberal education imparts a *sense of democracy*, engendering an inclination to participate in the democratic process, to accept the outcome of that process as legitimate, and to adjust one's behaviour to facilitate collective rule. The emphasis these programmes place on academic community supports the development of this democratic disposition.

Obviously, all the features of an educational model work together, and one should not look at these virtues, or the educational strategies that promote them, in isolation. However, together these features explain the civic potential of liberal education. By exploring them, an agenda for higher education will emerge that points the way to reforms that would make the teaching of civic virtue a more central part of university education in Europe. The concluding chapter will present this agenda and consider several strategies for its implementation.

The education one generation gives the next will shape society in all kinds of ways, for better or for worse. If we wish to ensure that our children inherit flourishing democracies that are able to deal with the challenges of the future, we must teach them how to make those democracies work. We cannot, as we often do, simply assume that they will know how to do so, and then lament when they face difficulties. Rather, we must consciously educate them to meet the high expectations that democratic governance places on citizens. LAS education can remind higher education that it should educate free citizens and can point the way on how to do this.

# Notes

1 Aristotle, *Politics*, 1310ª12 (Adapted from a translation by William Ellis).
2 See Bruce Kimball, *Orators & Philosophers: A History of the Idea of Liberal Education* (New York: Teachers College Press, 1986).
3 There is an important discussion to be had about the differences between multidisciplinarity, interdisciplinarity, and transdisciplinarity in academic curricula. However, for present purposes, the term multidisciplinarity will be used to refer broadly to any curriculum that combines different academic disciplines.
4 Colin Woodard, "Eastern European Academics Make the Case for the Liberal Arts," *The Chronicle of Higher Education*, November 15, 1996.
5 Teun Dekker, "Liberal Arts in Europe," in *Encyclopedia of Educational Philosophy and Theory*, ed. Michael Peters (Singapore: Springer, 2017).
6 For a count that was accurate as of summer 2019, see Daniel Kontowski, "European Liberal Education, 1990–2015: A Critical Exploration of Commonality in the Visions of Eight First Leaders" (PhD diss., University of Winchester, 2020), 167–72.
7 See, for example, European Students Union, *Bologna with Student Eyes: The Final Countdown* (Brussels, 2018); Michael Gaebel et al., *Learning and Teaching in the European Higher Education Area* (Brussels: European University Association, 2018).
8 Three research publications were also written based on these data, dealing with how students experience freedom of choice, how they learn critical thinking, and how their education prepares them for the labour market. See Teun Dekker, "Teaching Critical Thinking through Engagement with Multiplicity," *Thinking Skills and Creativity* 37 (2020); Teun Dekker, "The Value of Curricular Choice through Student Eyes," *The Curriculum Journal* 32, no. 2 (2021); Teun Dekker, "Generic Skills Development in European Liberal Arts and Sciences Programmes: A Student Perspective," (Forthcoming). Five quotes from those papers reappear here, albeit in a different context and for a different audience.
9 Accidentally and regrettably omitted in previous publications drawing on this dataset.

# References

Dekker, Teun. "Liberal Arts in Europe." In *Encyclopedia of Educational Philosophy and Theory*, edited by Michael Peters. Singapore: Springer, 2017.
Dekker, Teun. "Teaching Critical Thinking through Engagement with Multiplicity." *Thinking Skills and Creativity* 37 (2020): 100701.
Dekker, Teun. "The Value of Curricular Choice through Student Eyes." *The Curriculum Journal* 32, no. 2 (2021): 198–214.
Dekker, Teun. "Generic Skills Development in European Liberal Arts and Sciences Programmes: A Student Perspective." (Forthcoming).
European Students Union. *Bologna with Student Eyes: The Final Countdown*. Brussels, 2018.
Gaebel, Michael, Thérèse Zhang, Luisa Bunescu, and Henriette Stoeber. *Learning and Teaching in the European Higher Education Area*. Brussels: European University Association, 2018.

Kimball, Bruce. *Orators & Philosophers: A History of the Idea of Liberal Education.* New York: Teachers College Press, 1986.

Kontowski, Daniel. "European Liberal Education, 1990–2015: A Critical Exploration of Commonality in the Visions of Eight First Leaders." PhD diss., University of Winchester, 2020.

Woodard, Colin. "Eastern European Academics Make the Case for the Liberal Arts." *The Chronicle of Higher Education*, November 15, 1996, A55.

# 2 Civic Virtue, Democracy, and Democratic Conversations

Almost everyone has an intuitive idea of what it means to be a good citizen in a democracy. One should have at least some interest in social affairs as well as a willingness to participate in the democratic process, and one should probably not only be concerned with one's self-interest. However, these platitudes are too general to base an educational agenda on. Considering how education can contribute to the cultivation of civic virtue requires a more fully defined conception of citizenship. Any such conception must itself be grounded in a particular conception of democracy and the role civic virtue plays within it. This chapter will begin by examining the nature of virtue and of civic virtue, showing why it is important in democratic governance. It will then explore the concept of democracy and present a conception of the role citizens should play within it, which will be the basis of the seven democratic virtues of liberal education discussed in this book.

Democracy is a complicated and contested concept. The basic idea is that democracy is rule by the people, but there are many different conceptions of how rule by the people is supposed to work. Each conception is based on a different understanding of how exactly citizens should shape governmental decisions. Despite this, this chapter argues that one can identify five core values that are inherent to the concept of democracy and that any reasonable conception of democracy can endorse. A basic model of democratic interaction will then be sketched, which revolves around the idea of a democratic conversation. This is a special kind of conversation, one in which the five basic democratic values are realised. For this conversation to be successful, participants must display certain virtues. Without them, a democratic conversation degenerates into a different kind of conversation, one that does not live up to democratic ideals. It will then be shown how this kind of conversation is implicit in many contemporary democratic processes, and in all kinds of social interactions. Hence, the virtues that are required to sustain democracy are the virtues that help citizens navigate these democratic conversations. As such, the concept of a democratic conversation mediates

DOI: 10.4324/9781003336594-2

between the five fundamental democratic values on the one hand and the seven democratic virtues on the other. These virtues are the basis of an agenda for civic education, on which later chapters will elaborate.

## Civic Virtue in Democracy

At its most basic, a virtue is a characteristic of an entity, be it a person or object, which is beneficial for a certain purpose. Sharpness is a virtue in a knife because it is something that helps knives cut well. Similarly, loyalty is a virtue in a friend, because it is a trait that makes one a better friend. In thinking about human virtues, there are three elements to note. Firstly, in a virtue, the characteristic in question is a disposition to act in a certain way and the possession of skills, competencies, or knowledge that facilitate this. As such, a virtue is a character trait, an inclination that is connected to one's identity and that shows itself in how one behaves. A loyal friend is someone who tends to support friends, even if doing so is costly or difficult, both because they want to do so and because they have the abilities required. It is worth noting that there are dispositional and instrumental virtues. Dispositional virtues are concerned with having certain intentions or values. They denote having a desire to behave in a certain way that one typically acts on. For example, courage denotes a willingness not to shirk from conflicts or difficult situations. Other virtues are more instrumental in nature. They refer to having certain abilities, including, for example, resourcefulness or ingenuity. Those who possess these virtues are able to find creative solutions to difficult problems. Of course, this typology is a matter of emphasis. Courageous people are also able to act on their courage, while resourceful individuals also typically seek to use their abilities to solve problems. Nevertheless, it is important to note that both dispositional and instrumental properties can be virtues.

Secondly, virtues denote a certain degree of excellence in these characteristics; to say that one possesses a certain virtue is to say that one possesses a beneficial or admirable characteristic and does so to a high degree. Cowardice is not a virtue, because, by definition, it is not a good thing to have. Nor would one call those who only sometimes seek to tell the truth honest. Of course, virtues are a matter of degree, and one need not realise them to the highest degree to possess them. Even the most loyal of friends sometimes let their acquaintances down. Despite this, those who are said to have certain virtues must possess the relevant characteristics to a noteworthy extent.

Thirdly, virtues are relative to particular purposes. A characteristic is a virtue because it is beneficial to some ideal. Comfort is a virtue in deskchairs because this makes them good for sitting in, which is the purpose of such chairs. In traditional thinking about human virtues, as derived from

Aristotle,[1] the purpose in question is often defined as human flourishing, or *eudaimonia*, a particular normative conception of what it means to live a valuable existence. However, virtues might also relate to more specific human purposes. In the context of social affairs, it is helpful to think about these purposes as social roles, i.e., conceptions of how individuals in certain positions should behave to fulfil those roles well. Fairness of judgment is a virtue in a judge because it helps them live up to the expectations society has of judges. Similarly, dexterity with a knife is a virtue in a cook because it helps the cook do the things that a cook should do well. This makes discussions about social virtues unabashedly normative; they rely on ideals of what certain roles entail and what it takes to do them well. As such, those who have different conceptions of particular social roles will have different understandings of what it means to fulfil them well, and, as a consequence, prize different virtues. For example, some think that lawyers should seek to advance the interests of their clients at all costs, and, for them, aggressiveness would be a virtue, while others believe that good lawyers should seek to find fair solutions, which would lead them to value the ability to find compromise as a virtue. To argue for why a particular characteristic should be considered a virtue, one must first specify the particular purpose or, in the case of social virtues, the social role to which the virtue relates, explain what it entails and what it means to fulfil it well, before showing how the characteristic serves that purpose or role.

Following this analysis, civic virtues are those characteristics, whether they be skills, dispositions, competencies, or attitudes, that members of a society require to fulfil their roles in the political system well. Any political system specifies a range of positions and roles that members of society occupy, including what their functions are, what powers they have, and how they relate to other groups. This provides a normative ideal of how the political system is to work, and of what it means for people in different positions to do their jobs well, relative to which various virtues can be defined. In his *Republic*, for example, the ancient philosopher Plato, perhaps the staunchest critic of democracy and the most eloquent advocate of authoritarian government, proposed a political system that distinguishes between three social classes: the guardians, the auxiliaries, and, the largest group, the common people. Each of these classes has a specific function. The guardians make decisions for the community as a whole, the auxiliaries carry out these decisions and protect the state from external threats, and the people follow these decisions, producing the goods the state needs to sustain itself.[2] For this system to work well, each class needs to fulfil its function properly, and this requires certain virtues. The guardians must be wise and concerned with the public good, the auxiliaries must be brave and strong, and the common people need to be temperate and obedient.

Civic virtue matters in a political system because if members of society do not fulfil their roles in the political system well, the system will not work as intended, resulting in sub-optimal outcomes. To continue with Plato's proposed system, if the rulers are not concerned with the public good, they will not make decisions that are optimal for the community. Likewise, if the common people question the decisions of the rulers, the rulers will be less effective and the common people will be distracted from producing, to the detriment of all. Indeed, it is the decline of civic virtue that Plato identifies as the cause of the eventual demise of his system of government.[3]

Democratic governance works very differently, denying the existence of a superior class of people who are uniquely suited to rule. However, it too specifies different roles for actors in the political process. This means that it also requires citizens to display civic virtue. Indeed, in a democracy, the role that citizens play is more complex than in many other government systems, making it harder to fulfil and requiring more in the way of preparation. Moreover, since citizens are expected to be relatively involved in democratic governance, there are many opportunities for them not to carry out their role well, making democracy inherently fragile. As such, civic virtue is particularly important in democracies.

The importance of civic virtue has been emphasised throughout the history of democratic theory. As was noted in Chapter 1, it is a key insight in Aristotle's discussion of democracy. Modern democratic theorists have also stressed its importance. Jürgen Habermas famously noted that "the institutions of constitutional freedom are only worth as much as a population makes of them."[4] Perhaps the most systematic advocate for the importance of civic virtue in a democracy is William Galston, who presented an elaborate account of the role it plays in democratic governance.[5] Similarly, Stephen Macedo showed that even a liberal democracy, with its strong emphasis on neutrality towards different conceptions of the good, cannot function without some shared conception of the civic virtues citizens are to display.[6]

Because of the central role civic virtue plays in any democracy, many of the pathologies that plague democratic societies can be understood as failures of civic virtue. Moreover, many of the challenges that democracies face can only be met if citizens fulfil their role in the best possible way. Consider some of the most pressing issues that affect European democracies.

It has been argued that political polarisation is one of the biggest problems that European democracies face. Increasingly, citizens support far-right and far-left political movements, and their allegiances are becoming so entrenched that meaningful debate between the various factions is becoming much harder, and compromise is almost impossible. As a result, there seems to be a coarsening of the political discourse and less good-faith debate about the most important issues affecting society. Obviously, politicians and the media play a part in these phenomena, but at their root lies the fact that citizens are not willing to exchange views with those who have different opinions, reconsider their own positions, and find common ground. They also seem to be swayed by vacuous rhetoric and do not seek out high-quality political debate. If more citizens were more fair-minded, interested in other perspectives, and open to compromise, as well as more discerning in how they engage with political debates, extremist political movements and purveyors of low-quality political discourse would not be as successful. More civic virtue would certainly contribute to reducing political polarisation.

Relatedly, there is a widely shared concern about the influence of so-called fake news over the democratic process, especially in the context of social media, whose algorithms can create filter bubbles that limit the kinds of information people are presented with. Fake news, i.e., deliberately inaccurate items of news that seek to shape citizens' opinions, is particularly problematic when used by foreign governments to promote disunity and improperly influence the democratic process. While citizens cannot be held responsible for the existence of fake news, the reason it influences them is that many do not realise, or do not wish to realise, that it is fake. If they were more critical of the news they see, reflected more on the sources of the information they consume, and actively sought out news that offers perspectives different from their own, fake news would not get very much traction, and foreign intervention in the democratic process would not pose a threat. Here, too, more civic virtue would make a difference.

Similarly, proponents of democracy often worry about the rise of authoritarian governments that seek to restrict the rule of law or muzzle the media and that do not respect the fundamental rights of all citizens, especially minorities, thereby violating the democratic norm of equality. Such governments depend on the support of large numbers of citizens, who vote for them and do not protest *en masse*. But if most citizens correctly understood the intentions of authoritarian political movements, refused to vote for parties that are not committed to equality, and actively protested governments that do not respect the rule of law, authoritarianism would be less of a concern.

Even democracies that function well still face huge challenges that can only be met if citizens display the appropriate civic virtues. For example, combatting climate change or reducing social and economic inequality can only be achieved through concerted, long-term measures that might very well be detrimental to many in the short term. That is why some have doubted whether democratic societies can deal with these challenges, as citizens would never support measures that impose high costs in the short run and only yield tangible benefits many years later. Acting effectively against climate change and inequality in a democracy will require citizens to recognise the importance of these matters and accept measures that go against their immediate self-interest. This will demand considerable civic virtue.

It is important not to overemphasise the importance of civic virtue. One can hardly explain everything that is wrong with contemporary democracy by pointing to a lack of relevant skills and attitudes in the citizenry. Material circumstances, class dynamics, institutional failure, bad luck, political intrigue, and many other factors all play a part. Nor should one assume that if only citizens played their role in the democratic process well, heaven on earth would soon manifest itself. However, how citizens play their part in the democratic process matters. There are few wrongs within democratic societies that a bit more civic virtue could not, at the very least, make better.

## Five Basic Democratic Values

To determine which particular civic virtues citizens should possess, one must first consider the nature of democracy, starting from its most basic concept and fundamental values. One might begin by observing that human beings do not live solitary existences. Rather, they live together in communities and are bound by shared ways of living. This makes possible many benefits, such as a division of labour, leading to economic, technical, and cultural development, but it also allows for valuable social relationships and the cultivation of individual identity. Sustaining a community requires shared rules about a range of issues, ranging from what individuals can or must do, to how the burdens and benefits of social cooperation will be shared. Without such rules, society cannot function, and the benefits of communal existence will not materialise. Communities are also faced with challenges and threats, as well as opportunities, and must decide how to respond to these. Hence, any community requires a system of governance, i.e., a way of deciding what the rules are and how to deal with issues that arise. Communities can make decisions in many ways. The basic idea of democracy is that the members of the community should rule themselves and collectively decide on questions of governance. Implicit in this simple idea are five values: freedom, equality, the common good, legitimacy, and popular participation.

Firstly, the basic assumption of democratic governance is that the people of a community are free, in the sense that they may decide for themselves what to think and how to live their lives within the rules of that community.[7] How they exercise their freedom matters, and their views and choices demand respect; they cannot simply be ignored. As a result, the community will be characterised by a great deal of diversity. Different people will have different conceptions of how to live their lives and what is to their advantage. But they will also have different ideas about what the rules of the community should be, what the biggest challenges facing that community are, and how these are to be addressed. Their different choices and circumstances will result in them having different perspectives, which shape what they believe to be beneficial for their communities.

A system of governance that does not respect the freedom of individuals cannot be considered properly democratic. If a government does not allow citizens to decide for themselves how they wish to live or what to think but forces this upon them, the government controls the citizens, the citizens do not control the government. It is true that any government must, in some sense, constrain citizens. Such is the nature of rules. However, the governance process should incorporate different perspectives to be truly democratic. Dismissing certain opinions outright is unacceptable precisely because of people's right to have their own views on matters. Of course, it may be the case that certain views are undemocratic in nature because they would deny other people their freedom or are otherwise opposed to the democratic process. These anti-democratic views can be excluded from the process of governance. This is often thought of as a paradox, but it is inherent in the concept of democracy. A system of governance predicated on freedom cannot allow that freedom to be denied. If it does, it abolishes itself. Where exactly the boundary between acceptable freedom of speech and anti-democratic speech lies is a difficult matter that is much discussed, but few would contest that there is such a border. Indeed, almost all contemporary democracies have some limits on anti-democratic perspectives.

Secondly, in a democracy, citizens regard each other as having equal intrinsic worth and believe that all members of the community should be treated as equals. All should count for one. This does not deny the fact that there are significant differences between individuals or require that everyone is treated the same in all cases. But it does demand that all individuals' interests are given full and equal consideration. No one has an inherent right to have their needs and desires take priority over those of others. A society that does accord an individual such a right effectively creates a hierarchy in which some permanently rule over others. If one's rights count for more, one has a greater share of the ruling power, at the expense of others. This is undemocratic. Here, too, some caveats need to be made. Not everyone's interests can be optimally served at the same time. Inevitably, rules and policies will benefit some more than others. Again, however, the process is important: democratic decision-making needs to give everyone's interests equal consideration and take everyone into account equally. How one does so is a difficult matter, but equality is nevertheless a fundamental democratic value.

Thirdly, and following from the previous values, decisions in a democracy should be taken in the interest of the common good. This is an ancient idea, originating with Aristotle, who, in his *Politics*, drew a distinction between perverted and righteous forms of government, based on whether the rulers make decisions in their self-interest or in the interest of all. Confusingly, while he reserved the term democracy for a perverted form of government, that of the rule of a bare majority in its own interest, what one would consider a democracy in the contemporary sense aims to make decisions that serve the community as a whole.[8] For the goal of democracy is not to benefit some at the expense of others, but rather to find solutions to social problems that do justice to all concerned. The concept of the common good is undoubtedly vague and can be understood in numerous ways. However, the ideal of democracy requires some idea of the common or social good, as a system of government that aims only at the benefit of a particular group or individual cannot be said to constitute rule by the people, but only rule by some people.

Not only must the decisions produced by a democratic system serve the common good, but they must also, fourthly, be legitimate. After all, since no system of governance will be able to coerce all members of the community into obeying the rules all the time, citizens must, in general, accept those rules and policies as binding and have reason to believe that they have an obligation to follow them. Of course, some individuals may break the rules from time to time or deny that they need to follow the rules at all, but if large numbers of people do so, social cooperation breaks down and does so at a considerable price, as the benefits of social cooperation will not materialise. Hence, democracy should function in such a way as to generate support for measures taken. For, in a democratic society, governance ultimately depends on the support of the people. Measures that are not seen as legitimate can hardly be justified as springing from the people.

Fifthly, democracy rests on the belief that the way to realise the other four values is through universal participation in the governance process. This can be organised in all kinds of ways, but it is essential to democracy that the people play some role in governing, whether directly through, for example, citizens' assemblies, or indirectly, usually by voting in elections. Participation in democracy is important for a number of reasons. For one thing, it can be designed to treat people as free and equal. By ensuring that all can participate regardless of their beliefs and interests, all perspectives can be included, respecting people's freedom. Furthermore, by ensuring that the process of participation treats all participants as equals, it can respect equality.

Participation is also central to democracy because it can lead to decisions that serve the common good, i.e., that are good decisions for the community. There is a tradition in democratic thought that decisions made by large groups of people are likely to be good decisions because they pool the wisdom of the masses. This is also a thought that finds its origin in Aristotle, who argued that even if most people are not as smart or well-educated as a governing elite might be, their wisdom and insight can be aggregated, resulting in better judgment than what a small group of experts can produce.[9] This insight was further developed by the 18th-century mathematician Condorcet.[10] His jury theorem states that the likelihood of a group of people making a correct assessment, in a matter where there is an objectively correct answer, depends both on their probability of being right, which may be understood as their expertise, and the number of people in the group. When the number of individuals involved is very large, the likelihood of arriving at a correct decision becomes very high. Of course, one cannot involve an entire political community in every decision, but regarding important and difficult issues, it might well be worth involving everyone, perhaps through referenda and the like.

Aristotle also argues that all members of a political community are equal in their ability to judge whether a government composed of qualified experts is doing a good job.[11] He replies to Plato that one might not be an expert at something but still be able to judge the quality of the work of experts. For example, one might not be able to prepare food of the highest quality, but one can determine if one likes the food that an expert chef has produced. So, too, one might have no idea how to design and operate a mass-transit system, but almost everyone can form an opinion about whether it functions well. A system of governance that allows citizens to participate, even if only to indicate whether they approve of the work of the government, is likely to result in decisions that, in the judgement of the people, function well for society as a whole.

Lastly, participation is key to ensuring that decisions are perceived as legitimate by the people. After all, if the governing process allows everyone to participate, the people are, in some sense, the authors of those decisions. When they obey those decisions, they obey themselves, and so they have a very good reason to accept them as binding.

However, for all these benefits to materialise, participation must have a certain character. To understand this character, it is useful to consider the work of the French philosopher Jean-Jacques Rousseau, and in particular the central argument in his *Of the Social Contract*.[12] In his theory, individuals who become members of a community submit themselves to the decisions of that community. However, in doing so, they also gain the right to shape those decisions. They do so by participating in the determination of the general will. The general will is a much-discussed concept, and Rousseau's description of it is hardly straightforward. However, one might plausibly understand it as the will of the community as a whole. It is based on an aggregation of each citizen's assessment of what is good for society. When

confronting a particular question, every member of society must independently ask what they believe is in the best interest of the community as a
whole. When all citizens express their views, they will converge on a joint
conclusion. The more unanimity there is, the more likely it is that the true
general will has been found, which is to say that the solution is indeed in
the best interest of the entire community. This gives one a strong reason
to accept it as binding. For if one initially believed that a particular course
of action was not in the best interest of the community, then the fact that a
substantial majority of people believe that it is provides reason to conclude
that one was wrong and to accept the decision of the majority as correct.
This would give one reason to regard it as legitimate.

Unfortunately, matters can go awry when citizens do not ask themselves
what is in the interest of the community as a whole, but rather what is beneficial for them personally. When citizens ask themselves that question,
the aggregation does not reveal the general will, but rather the will of all.
The will of all has no privileged status, being merely the aggregation of
individual self-interest. It is an artificial construct that represents nothing
that is of any democratic significance. If most people regard something as
not being in their self-interest, this does not give those in the minority any
reason to regard the decision as the best solution for the community as a
whole. Hence, one has no reason to regard the will of all as a legitimate
basis for binding norms in the same way that one can regard the general will
as a basis for authoritative rules. This makes it very important that citizens
ask themselves the right question when they participate in the democratic
process. Indeed, Rousseau goes as far as to argue that when individuals ask
themselves the wrong question, it is permissible to force them to comply
with the decision they would have reached had they asked themselves the
correct question, and to do so on the basis that that is what they want, if only
they would realise it. In this way, Rousseau claims "they can be forced to
be free."[13] This conception of governance, it must be said, has given rise to
concerns that it can lead to oppressive totalitarianism.[14] These concerns are
well-founded and should be guarded against. However, this does not undermine the insight that, when engaging in a deliberative democratic process,
it is important that citizens do not think about their self-interest, but rather
consider the advantage of society as a whole.

## Democratic Conversations

Imagine a small group of people who form a political community. They
are committed to the five basic values of democracy discussed above, and
they seek to make decisions in a way that realises those values. Inspired by
the classical ideal of direct democracy, they might gather in some central

place to have a conversation about the issues they face and to reach some sort of conclusion. This would have to be a special kind of conversation, a democratic conversation, governed by certain conventions and assumptions. After all, not all conversations incorporate the values of democracy. In some conversations, one person issues instructions to another. Other conversations are transactional, with participants seeking to exchange one thing for another. These are not democratic conversations.

For a conversation to be genuinely democratic, the basic rules of the conversation must reflect the fundamental values of democracy. All participants must regard each other as free and equal; they must accept that individuals may have different perspectives, interests, preferences, and opinions; and they must also accept that these differences are relevant to the conversation. Believing that some people do not have a right to their convictions or that they should count for less than others in the decision-making process is undemocratic. Moreover, participants must enter the conversation with the ambition to make decisions that serve the common good, rather than advance their private good. The goal is to arrive at the best solution for the community, rather than to claim as much as possible for oneself. Hence, decisions must be justified in ways that others can accept. To argue that a certain course of action is the correct one because it serves one's self-interest best is an argument that has little relevance for others. Rather, arguments should aim at interpersonal justification, i.e., they should appeal to shared interests and values. Only then can the community regard eventual decisions as its own, and, for that reason, as legitimate. Moreover, if no one participates in this conversation, nothing will happen and the process cannot be regarded as democratic. In sum, the goal of a democratic conversation is for the participants to make good decisions for the community, through a collective, collaborative exchange of perspectives. It is a shared process of discovery through which free and equal citizens shape their societies.

As such, democratic conversations are quite different from, for example, negotiations. In a negotiation, parties seek to advance their own, predetermined interests. They are not committed to the common good, and they do not regard the interests of others as on a par with their own. Nor are they particularly concerned with the perspectives of others except in a strategic sense, as understanding others' perspectives may help to improve their position in the negotiation. Democratic conversations are also quite different from conversations in which one party seeks to convince another party of something. In such a conversation, one party has already decided what the correct answer is and aims to convince the other party to accept it. Parties do not respect the legitimacy of other points of view or care about the interpersonal justifiability of whatever is decided. All that matters is whether they get their way. These kinds of conversations are effectively battles; they are competitions of wit and persuasion for domination or private gain. They are not cooperative explorations of shared problems by free and equal citizens seeking to find legitimate solutions that benefit the community as a whole. As such, they do not respect the fundamental values of democracy, and decisions that are reached through such conversations are not truly democratic. These decisions reflect differences in power, rhetorical skills, and negotiating position, not the collective deliberations of society.

Participants in democratic conversations need to ensure their conversations adhere to the values of freedom, equality, the common good, legitimacy, and popular participation. The moment they cease to regard other participants as free and equal, perhaps because they start to believe their interests should count for more than the interests of others or because they believe they have all the answers even before the conversation starts, the conversation ceases to be democratic. Similarly, if they no longer concern themselves with the interest of the community and start to consider what benefits them, or if they do not argue in ways that meet the requirements of interpersonal justification, the conversation also strays from democratic ideals.

Annoyingly, it can be quite difficult to ascertain whether a conversation is democratic. Democratic conversations can appear similar to other conversations, at least on the surface. Of course, if participants yell abuse, refuse to listen, or blatantly press their own advantage, something has obviously gone awry. However, oftentimes deviations from the ideal of a democratic conversation are more subtle. Seeking the common good or regarding others as free and equal are states of mind that are easily obscured. Even those involved in a conversation may be unsure whether they are participating while respecting democratic values. One might not be sure whether one advocates a certain policy because one genuinely regards it as beneficial for all or because it promises to benefit one's self-interest. Nor is it easy to know if one has considered the perspectives of others or dismissed them out of hand. Hence, it is crucial to be mindful of the nature of democratic conversations and to constantly reflect on whether the conversation one is having truly embodies the values of democracy.

The ideal of free and equal people meeting in a public forum to discuss issues of shared concern in accordance with democratic values is as appealing as it is distant from contemporary democratic practice. Almost no society uses this kind of direct democracy. Modern democratic systems are based on representatives, elected by citizens, who pass legislation and hold governments to account. These representatives do their work in the context of a public sphere of political discourse in which the issues facing society are debated. This public sphere is sustained by freedom of expression, freedom of association, freedom of protest, and a free press. The political discourse that takes place in this public sphere, whether it occurs in legislative assemblies or through the media, in some way informs the voting behaviour of ordinary citizens. Nevertheless, most citizens only contribute by taking in political discourse, usually by reading the newspapers, watching TV, or following social media, and then voting in elections. Although they may occasionally discuss current issues within their social circles, they do not participate in face-to-face conversations about governance, democratic or otherwise, in any obvious sense.

However, despite the fact that in contemporary democracy most citizens play a limited political role, the ways in which they participate in the governance of their societies should resemble a democratic conversation in spirit. Political discourse in the public sphere is a conversation in some sense, in that different parties put forth perspectives on issues of social concern and respond to each other's contributions. This is an exchange of views that leads to decisions being taken in the political arena and can be regarded as a conversation. Although most citizens do not participate in these conversations, they do observe them from a distance and base their own political actions on what they hear, even if these are confined to voting. This is not that different from more direct forms of democracy. Even in the smallest direct democracy, most citizens who attend assemblies do not speak much. Rather, they listen to the contributions of a few speakers and indicate their approval or disapproval of certain proposals. Citizens in modern democracies do likewise, albeit in more mediated ways. In this way, modern politics can still be characterised as a conversation. For it to be democratic, it must be conducted with the same attitudes and assumptions that characterise more recognisable democratic conversations. Those who do participate actively in the political discourse should seek to realise the fundamental values of democracy in their contributions. Moreover, citizens must, in observing the discourse, reflecting on it, and deciding how to vote, seek to adhere to the fundamental values of democracy as well. For example, in deciding what they think about certain social problems, they must respect differences of opinion and consider the interests of all citizens. In deciding which party to vote for, they should have some regard for the interest of the community as they understand it, and they should not be moved by arguments that are not based on shared interests and values.

If governance is not conducted in accordance with the norms of democratic conversations, it does not realise the fundamental values of democracy. Instead, it becomes a form of governance that might resemble democracy in an institutional sense, with parliaments and elections, but that has none of the benefits of democracy. If political discourse is riddled with racism, it can hardly be said to treat all citizens as equals. If certain opinions are marginalised and excluded, freedom is not respected. Similarly, if citizens vote only based on what serves them best, outcomes are not likely to benefit the community at large and can hardly be regarded as legitimate by others. Lastly, if citizens do not participate, the conversation does not belong to them, and cannot be considered democratic.

Nor is the importance of democratic conversations limited to the formal political process. Whenever individuals come together as free and equal people to achieve some goal they cannot realise on their own, they are effectively engaging in some sort of democratic conversation. This applies within families, but also in civic associations, clubs, and certain working environments. As in a political community, members must make collective decisions, and the diverse nature of their associations dictates that they cannot do so without respecting each other's interests, insights, and individual perspectives. Nor can they press their own advantage at the expense of others. If they do not interact in the spirit of the association, its character changes, sometimes subtly, sometimes dramatically. It will fail to live up to its highest purpose, to the detriment of all.

Thinking of proper democratic interaction in terms of a democratic conversation helps specify what political role citizens should play in society: a good citizen is someone who participates in democratic conversations well, i.e., someone who, in their political behaviour, engages with others in accordance with the norms that govern democratic conversations. The civic virtues that citizens should acquire to play their role effectively are the skills, abilities, and dispositions that contribute to this conversation remaining democratic and not degenerating into an altogether different kind of conversation. These are the virtues that one generation should seek to instil in the next. Advancing an educational agenda for this purpose requires demonstrating that it cultivates traits which contribute to the ability to participate in democratic conversations.

## Notes

1  For Aristotle's discussion of the concept of virtue, see Aristotle, *Nicomachean Ethics*.
2  Plato, *Republic*, book 2–3.
3  Plato, *Republic*, book 8.
4  Jürgen Habermas, "Citizenship and National Identity: Some Reflections on the Future of Europe," *Praxis International* 12, no. 1 (1992): 7.
5  William Galston, *Liberal Purposes: Goods, Virtues, and Diversity in the Liberal State* (Cambridge: Cambridge University Press, 1991).
6  Stephen Macedo, *Liberal Virtues: Citizenship, Virtue, and Community in Liberal Constitutionalism* (Oxford: Oxford University Press, 1990).
7  There is, of course, the matter of who counts as a member of the community. This is a separate issue that has been the subject of much debate. For present purposes, it will be stipulated that a fixed community exists and that all members of that community are full citizens.

8  Aristotle, *Politics*, book 3, chapter 7.
9  Aristotle, *Politics*, book 3, chapter 11.
10  Marquis de Condorcet, *Essay on the Application of Analysis to the Probability of Majority Decisions.*
11  Aristotle, *Politics*, book 3, chapter 11.
12  Jean-Jacques Rousseau, *Of the Social Contract*, book 4.
13  Jean-Jacques Rousseau, *Of the Social Contract*, book 1, chapter 7.
14  See Isaiah Berlin, *Two Concepts of Liberty* (London: Routledge, 2017).

# References

Berlin, Isaiah. *Two Concepts of Liberty*. London: Routledge, 2017.

Galston, William. *Liberal Purposes: Goods, Virtues, and Diversity in the Liberal State*. Cambridge: Cambridge University Press, 1991.

Habermas, Jürgen. "Citizenship and National Identity: Some Reflections on the Future of Europe." *Praxis International* 12, no. 1 (1992): 1–19.

Macedo, Stephen. *Liberal Virtues: Citizenship, Virtue, and Community in Liberal Constitutionalism*. Oxford: Oxford University Press, 1990.

# 3 Teaching Civic Virtue in Universities

The importance of civic virtue to the functioning of democracy makes its cultivation in future generations a matter of great concern. No one is born with the skills and dispositions required to be a good citizen. The relevant abilities and attitudes are remarkably complex and require high-level cognitive functioning. Developing these requires a multifaceted and long process of socialisation in a range of different venues. How parents raise their children plays an important role. However, with families being both smaller and less diverse than societies, relying on families to instil civic virtue is unlikely to be sufficient. Moreover, a society cannot leave the development of civic virtue to the discretion of parents, as some parents might not, for whatever reason, teach their children the relevant skills and attitudes. Nor is the family an optimal environment for acquiring virtues that are inherently social.

That is why the cultivation of civic virtue should be a prime concern of formal education. After all, like society at large, schools are communities in which groups of relatively diverse people come together for mutual benefit. That makes them ideal venues for developing the skills and attitudes that are required to eventually participate in society. Moreover, the goal of education is to prepare students for their futures and help them develop the competencies that they will need to lead meaningful and productive lives. Since part of living a productive life in a democracy is participating in the democratic process, almost all European societies make the development of civic virtue a goal of their education systems.

However, efforts to cultivate civic virtue tend to focus on primary and secondary education. In most of Europe, the idea that higher education should also contribute to the development of civic virtue is not widely accepted. Higher education in Europe is highly diverse, and it is difficult to generalise about many hundreds of institutions in dozens of countries. But overall, universities focus on providing students with a scientific and academic education. Despite this, higher education has enormous potential

DOI: 10.4324/9781003336594-3

to contribute to the development of students' civic capacities. Of course, the groundwork must be laid before that time, so teaching civic virtue in primary and secondary education is necessary but not sufficient for realising the full potential of democracy.

This chapter will present an argument for making teaching civic virtue a key aim of higher education, based on a general conception of its purpose. Some might be sceptical of this argument because they deny the general conception of education presented or argue that it does not apply to higher education. Alas, it is difficult to prove the superiority of one conception of education over another. However, it is possible to show the limitations of arguments that might be made against the idea of universities teaching civic virtue. One might distinguish between democratic objections, which flow from a particular understanding of democracy, and academic objections, which are based on a specific conception of the university. By showing that these objections can be overcome, the chapter will buttress the claim that higher education both can and should help students cultivate the civic virtues they will need to be good citizens.

## Civic Virtue in Education

As a starting point for arguing why universities should, amongst other things, teach civic virtue, one might hold that education should prepare future generations for contributing to the community. It should equip students with the knowledge, skills, and attitudes required to fulfil the various roles they will play in society. That makes education different from training. Training, such as taking specific courses in the context of one's job or to learn a hobby, is relative to a specific, narrow purpose. However, education has wider goals, especially in the context of publicly regulated and supported education. It is concerned with the development of the person, and while it may have specific aims, such as preparing one for a particular job, this is never its only goal. As such, in setting out an educational agenda, one must ask what students will probably need to be able to do well in the future in a multitude of contexts, and then ask what dispositions, skills, and abilities they will need to do those things effectively. From this, one can deduce what they should be taught. For example, since students will be expected to be economically productive, it is important to ensure they are qualified to participate in the economic system. This requires them to be able to read, have certain subject-specific knowledge, understand that it is important to show up on time, and a whole host of other things. These can then be considered within the purview of the education system.

In a democracy, future generations will be expected to participate in the political process. After all, this participation is implicit in the idea of democracy as collective self-governance over time. One generation gradually hands over a political system to the next, and it does so in part by transmitting norms of citizenship. Hence, the theory of education sketched out above also requires that education teach students what they need to know and be able to do to act in accordance with those norms.

Although this conception of the role of education sounds straightforward, it is important to note its broad scope; if the goal of education is to prepare students for the roles they will need to play in society, it must go beyond merely teaching them practical skills and knowledge relevant to their future professions. While these are valuable, they are not enough to perform different social roles well. Being able to function in certain contexts also requires particular dispositions and inclinations, i.e., a certain character. Character can be understood as "a set of personal traits or dispositions that produce specific moral emotions, inform motivation, and guide conduct."[1] In turn, one's conduct determines how well one can function in different settings. Hence, education should always include an element of so-called character education. While there are many different conceptions of character education, they are united in the belief that:

> Because of the foundational role of the virtues in human flourishing, schools have a responsibility to cultivate the virtues, define and list those they want to prioritise, and integrate them into all teaching and learning, in and out of school.[2]

Character education is somewhat controversial. Some associate it with religious or conservative conceptions of education that seek to indoctrinate students with traditional values and respect for authority. Others view it with suspicion because they believe it promotes individual autonomy at the expense of community.[3] However, it is important to distinguish between the concept of character education and its content, i.e., the specific virtues that should be taught. Those who are critical of character education must ask themselves whether their objections pertain to the idea that education should help students develop their character or, rather, to the specific virtues being promoted. In many cases, the controversy relates to the content of character education, and the critics would not object to the teaching of a different conception of virtue that is more to their liking.

To avoid such controversy, it is crucial to justify the particular virtues that character education should promote in a way that can command widespread agreement. In a plural society, in which there are very different ideas about how one should live and which traits are virtuous, this is difficult. For this reason, a lot of research has sought to define a conception of virtue that is acceptable throughout a multicultural society.[4] However, this is less of an issue for civic virtue in the context of democratic governance than it is for other types of virtue. After all, in democratic societies, there is some agreement about the nature of the political process that future citizens are expected to participate in. Regular elections and universal suffrage, for example, are integral to how the system is supposed to work. With such a system come traits that citizens require to function well in it, and these virtues can be legitimately taught in the education system while avoiding controversy. One may disagree whether rebelliousness or chastity are virtues in a life well-lived, but the virtues associated with democracy, such as public-spiritedness or political engagement, are beneficial for all citizens in their political activities. This is not to say that there can be no disagreement about what role citizens should play in such a system or which virtues facilitate this role. But, insofar as a society regards itself as democratic, it must accept the character that facilitates democracy as virtuous.

Of course, it is easier to show that the education system as a whole should teach civic virtue than it is to show that civic virtue should be a concern of higher education specifically. To make this argument, one also needs to postulate what specific sectors of the education system – primary, secondary, and tertiary – should do. One might argue that each sector should focus on the cognitive capacities that students can develop at the age they participate in that education, but also that it should build on their previous education and experiences. This is why reading and writing should be taught in primary school. At that age, students are generally able to learn these skills well both in terms of their mental development and in light of their likely access to appropriate reading material. Calculus should be taught in secondary education, as it builds on basic numeracy skills developed in primary education, and the typical adolescent brain becomes capable of learning calculus around this time.

The skills required to have a democratic conversation, and, by extension, to participate effectively in the democratic process, are fairly high-level skills. As indicated in Chapter 2 and as will become clear in the following chapters, it demands a degree of reflectiveness, empathy, knowledge, and other competencies that most people only develop around the age they typically go to university. While these build on skills that one can develop earlier in one's life, mastering them to the level required can often only happen later. Indeed, psychological research reveals that students attend university right around the time their brains develop the higher-level cognitive capacities involved in the abstract, other-regarding reasoning that is central to democratic conversations.[5] Only from about 18 years of age can they learn certain civic virtues. So, while the basis for citizenship can be learnt in secondary or even primary school, this is unlikely to be enough.

Moreover, the circumstances in which most students find themselves when they go to university are particularly conducive to acquiring civic virtue. In many cases, students are confronted with more diversity than they have encountered before, making them more aware of the difficulties of living together that need to be overcome to make democracy work. They also often start living on their own and so acquire a greater degree of responsibility.

Around this time, students take on even more responsibility as they reach the legal age of majority, which comes with political rights, such as the right to vote. Furthermore, many students learn about social issues in their studies, and some become politically active. In sum, young people enter higher education at precisely the time they begin to take their first steps as full citizens in their political communities, and this seems like an opportune time to develop the skills required to participate in political life. Learning civic virtue around the time they gain independence and new rights enables them to apply what they have learned in a way that would be impossible as minors who are dependent on their parents. Although many valuable lessons can be imparted well before students attend university, some important things can only be taught when one's circumstances allow one to appreciate them.

There is a long tradition of arguing that higher education has a role to play in the cultivation of civic virtue. The philosopher Martha Nussbaum has passionately argued that university education should focus on teaching students the skills required for participation in the democratic process. Her *Cultivating Humanity*[6] and her *Not for Profit – Why Democracy Needs the Humanities*[7] explore how different university subjects and educational methods contribute to the development of several essential democratic skills. Similarly, Amy Gutmann's *Democratic Education*[8] sees a special place for universities in promoting freedom of association and preparing future officeholders in a democracy. Former Harvard president Derek Bok argues, in his *Beyond the Ivory Tower*,[9] that universities should cultivate their students' capacities for moral reasoning. As there has been a lively debate about this issue,[10] more accounts of the role civic virtue should play in higher education have been advanced.[11] However, the idea that higher education should promote civic virtue in students has existed since the rise of the modern university, running through John Dewey's *Democracy and Education*[12] as well as the work of John Henry Newman.

Some universities acknowledge that their function includes teaching their students certain civic virtues, at least in their public communications. Their mission statements and strategic plans include references to helping students become global citizens, enabling them to contribute to society, and allowing them to have a positive impact on their communities.[13] Moreover, policymakers and governments increasingly recognise that meeting the challenges of the future and sustaining democracy will require higher education to prepare students for their civic futures. For example, in 2018, the education ministers of the European Higher Education Area (EHEA) issued a communiqué calling for universities to "play a stronger social, cultural, and leadership role and foster social cohesion by providing students with values, skills, and aptitudes that promote civic participation, social inclusion, sustainability, and global citizenship."[14] Similar calls have been issued in individual European countries, and by various agencies of the European Union.[15] There is thus a wide coalition in favour of universities making the cultivation of civic virtue more central to their educational mission.

## Democratic Objections

As simple as the argument that higher education should play a part in helping students become good citizens may sound, it is open to a number of objections. Some of these are rooted in the very nature of democracy. While it may sound paradoxical that there might be democratic objections to teaching civic virtue, doing so in universities raises a number of complications. For example, one might argue that teaching civic virtue within universities is an elitist project. After all, not everyone goes to university. Teaching citizenship skills in tertiary education suggests that only those who attend university can be good citizens. Indeed, it is often those who are already well-off who attend university, making fully functioning citizenship the preserve of the wealthy and well-connected. This violates the fundamental norm of equality that underlies democracy; in a democracy, all adults can and should participate, and so teaching civic virtue to only a part of the population is inappropriate. Perhaps this made sense in the past when political rights were only extended to a minority of the population. However, it is unbecoming of a modern, egalitarian society. Rather, civic virtue should be taught in primary and secondary education, as these are generally compulsory for all young people.

Needless to say, equality is indeed fundamental to democracy, and all citizens, regardless of their education levels, can and should be able to participate. However, teaching civic virtue in universities need not contradict this. Firstly, in a modern democracy, the right to participate is not conditional on demonstrating that one is in any way qualified to participate. Nor is there any suggestion that those who have gone to university should have additional political rights, such as being granted extra votes, for which John Stuart Mill famously argued.[16] Secondly, arguing that universities should teach civic virtue does not imply that they should have a monopoly on democratic education. It is both possible and highly desirable for civic virtue to be taught in other venues as well. It can and should be taught in secondary education, as mentioned above. It should also be included in vocational and professional education.

Moreover, citizens can also learn civic virtues in informal venues, most notably by participating in democracy. It is by seeing how some participate that other people can learn how to do so effectively; if one sees many proper democratic conversations, one is socialised into the process of engaging in them. That is why political communities need to ensure that they have a democratic culture in which the relevant virtues are clearly present. Teaching civic virtue in universities can contribute to such a democratic culture. The democratic virtues taught to some can rub off on others, and in that way benefit society as a whole. In many European nations, over 40% of young people receive tertiary education, and the European Union seeks to raise this to at least 45%.[17] As such, universities are not as exclusive as they once were, and their graduates can make a significant contribution to a political culture in which good citizenship is the norm. Of course, It is crucial to ensure access to universities for all members of society and to make sure those who do not go to university are also afforded opportunities to cultivate civic virtue. If this is done, then there is nothing elitist about making the teaching of civic virtue an aim of higher education.

A different democratic concern that one might have about teaching civic virtue in universities is that it politicises higher education. Under the guise of citizenship education, universities would indoctrinate their students with specific political perspectives. After all, many members of university communities have left-wing, progressive political perspectives, and the worry is that they would seek to transmit these to future generations. This might violate the fundamental value of freedom that underlies democracy, as it denies people the right to come to their own conclusions on political questions. Young students, who are in a relationship of dependence with their teachers, could easily be brainwashed into adopting certain views. These views would come to receive undue social prominence at the expense of other valid perspectives. In the extreme case, this could skew the democratic process, resulting in suboptimal decisions and the marginalisation of those with different opinions.

Certainly, any theory of civic education must be attentive to these concerns. However, it is important to distinguish two different ways in which education might be politicised. On the one hand, it might indeed seek to promote a particular political view. This would be inappropriate for democratic reasons, and it is something that a theory of civic education needs to avoid. However, education might also be politicised in the sense of being concerned with the political process, i.e., with teaching students how to participate in politics. This is not a violation of freedom, as the aim is to convey how to engage in democracy, not to promote specific political goals or opinions. If anything, this sort of political education is empowering, as it helps future citizens think for themselves, rather than indoctrinating them with particular viewpoints.

Of course, making a hard distinction between the political process and political substance is not as straightforward as it may seem, especially in the context of democracy. This is because democracy has both procedural and substantive aspects. While in most cases it simply prescribes a particular way of making decisions, its commitment to freedom and equality forbids outcomes that curtail these values. For example, democracy cannot unduly limit freedom of speech, institutionalise racism, or abolish the rule of law. Hence, it is not inappropriate for civic education to encourage freedom and equality; there is nothing undemocratic about promoting democracy.

The conception of democracy that was presented in the previous chapter is not politicised in the first sense of the word; it does not take a substantive position on political issues other than the ones that relate directly to the functioning of democracy. Rather, it arises out of the fundamental conditions of a group of citizens who regard each other as free and equal, who have diverse conceptions of their own good and of the common good, and who need to make collective choices for their futures that enjoy a high level of legitimacy. The democratic process, modelled in a particular conception of democratic conversations, is a way of achieving this. While it has some substantive components, it can hardly be described as liberal, conservative, or socialist. The seven virtues that allow citizens to participate in this conversation are similarly neutral. They do not favour a particular ideology but specify what is required to make social choices in the face of ideological diversity. As such, the conception of civic education that fosters these virtues is not unacceptably political.

## Academic Objections

Another kind of objection to civic education being part of universities is academic and starts from a conception of the role of universities. There is the view that university education should primarily be academic, focused on training future researchers or, if one insists, preparing students for professions that require an academic way of thinking, such as law or medicine. As a result, higher education should focus on teaching scientific knowledge and methods, as well as academic skills that will be useful for relevant professions. Civic education is better done in other contexts, whether it be in secondary education or in the context of social organisations such as fraternities, sororities, and student clubs. Teaching civic virtue crowds out what truly matters, as time spent on civic issues comes at the expense of scientific and academic development.[18]

Although many will find it impoverished, it is hard to provide a rigorous argument showing that this is an inaccurate understanding of the purpose of university education. However, several points can be made to nuance it.

For one thing, the reality is that only a small fraction of students become researchers, especially those studying at the Bachelor's and Master's levels. Even many people studying law do not become practising lawyers. Graduates end up pursuing all kinds of careers, especially in a rapidly changing labour market. Most of these will not require students to do academic research or use the scientific method. It seems problematic to base one's entire conception of higher education on the future careers of a minority of students.

Moreover, teaching civic virtue need not come at the expense of academic development. Perhaps if it were achieved through dedicated courses and lectures, there would be some crowding out. However, the features of the liberal education model that will be discussed in the following chapters for their value in promoting citizenship skills are also valuable for other reasons, including reasons of academic development. A multidisciplinary curriculum can promote open-mindedness, but it also allows for an academic understanding of complex problems. Similarly, an active pedagogy promotes cognitive development as well as independence of thought, while learning how to work in groups is beneficial in almost all professions. The civic curriculum presented here is woven into a curriculum that helps students achieve a range of other goals. The success of many graduates from LAS programmes, including those who went on to prestigious PhD programmes at research universities and successful academic careers, shows that education can effectively serve multiple goals at the same time.[19]

One might also object to teaching civic virtue in higher education on the grounds of academic freedom. If one were to argue that governments should force universities to teach civic virtue, this would be a threat to this freedom. After all, this fundamental value, which is central to the work of universities, holds that decisions about research and teaching should be made autonomously by academics for academic reasons. Interference by the state in setting the educational agenda would threaten the quality of teaching and research, as academics are best placed to make teaching and research decisions themselves. Governments simply lack the knowledge to make good choices, and they have an incentive to direct universities to serve their particular purposes, rather than to promote the autonomous development of science. Forcing higher education to focus on civic education may lead to bad teaching, as the government does not have the expertise to design a good curriculum. It also creates a real risk of governments seeking to promote their political ideologies by indoctrinating students. Moreover, it sets a dangerous precedent for official interference in other areas. If the government can direct university teaching, then why can it not also direct research, appointments, and governance decisions?

Academic freedom is indeed paramount for universities, and governmental interference with their operations is to be avoided at all costs. However, pursuing civic education need not come at the expense of academic freedom. For one thing, merely requiring or encouraging universities to teach civic virtue is different from specifying what competencies they should target or how these should be taught. In the same way that governments can, and often do, require higher education to prepare students for the labour market while leaving institutions free to determine their curricula, they might do the same in the case of civic education. In this way, qualified academic experts would still oversee the curriculum, ensuring both its quality and independence. This distinction between setting the goals of higher education and determining the means can also prevent a slippery slope into other forms of interference.

Furthermore, universities might decide for themselves that teaching civic virtue is an important part of their educational mission and do so for independent reasons. Academic freedom certainly does not prohibit institutions from engaging in civic education. This book seeks to provide reasons for them to do so; it aims to present a vision of the purpose of higher education in a democratic society and an agenda for civic education to realise it. Hopefully, that vision will persuade the higher education community that teaching civic virtue is a goal worth pursuing. In the end, there is no way of definitively refuting the claim that universities should only focus on scientific education. But, as is often remarked, it is better to show than to argue. The experiences of students in European LAS programmes are evocative; their reflections on their education paint a picture of what education could be. Some educators will not be moved by this picture, but others might find that it inspires them to make teaching civic virtue an integral part of their education and provides a model for doing so.

## Notes

1 Jubilee Centre for Character and Virtues, *A Framework for Character Education in Schools* (Birmingham: Jubilee Centre for Character and Virtues, University of Birmingham 2017), 2.
2 Ibid., 4.
3 For a discussion of these views, see Mark Pike, "Christianity and Character Education: Faith in Core Values?," *Journal of Beliefs & Values* 31, no. 3 (2010).
4 For example, see Stephen Macedo, *Diversity and Distrust: Civic Education in a Multicultural Democracy* (Cambridge, MA: Harvard University Press, 2009); Walter Feinberg, *Common Schools/Uncommon Identities: National Unity and Cultural Difference* (New Haven, CT: Yale University Press, 1998).
5 See Francis Jensen and Amy Nutt, *The Teenage Brain: A Neuroscientist's Survival Guide to Raising Adolescents and Young Adults* (New York: HarperCollins, 2015).

6  Martha Nussbaum, *Cultivating Humanity: A Classical Defense of Reform in Liberal Education* (Cambridge, MA: Harvard University Press, 1998).
7  Martha Nussbaum, *Not for Profit: Why Democracy Needs the Humanities* (Princeton, NJ: Princeton University Press, 2010).
8  Amy Gutmann, *Democratic Education* (Princeton, NJ: Princeton University Press, 1999).
9  Derek Bok, *Beyond the Ivory Tower* (Cambridge, MA: Harvard University Press, 1982).
10  See Elizabeth Kiss and J. Peter Euben, eds., *Debating Moral Education: Rethinking the Role of the Modern University* (Durham, NC: Duke University Press, 2010).
11  For example, see Kristján Kristjánsson, *Flourishing as the Aim of Education: A Neo-Aristotelian View* (London: Routledge, 2019); Rune Herheim, Tobias Werler, and Kjellrun Hiis Hauge, eds., *Lived Democracy in Education: Young Citizens' Democratic Lives in Kindergarten, School and Higher Education* (London: Routledge, 2021); Mark Halstead and Mark Pike, *Citizenship and Moral Education: Values in Action* (London: Routledge, 2006); Morgan White, *Towards a Political Theory of the University: Public Reason, Democracy, and Higher Education* (London: Routledge, 2016).
12  John Dewey, *Democracy and Education: An Introduction to the Philosophy of Education* (London: Macmillan, 1923).
13  For a discussion of these efforts, see Jubilee Centre for Character and Virtues and Oxford Character Project, *Character Education in Universities: A Framework for Flourishing* (Birmingham: University of Birmingham, 2020), 1.
14  EHEA Ministerial Conference, "Statement of the Fifth Bologna Policy Forum," *News Release*, 2018.
15  For example, see Luc van den Brande, *Reaching Out to EU Citizens—A New Opportunity* (Luxembourg: Publications Office of the European Union, 2017).
16  See John Stuart Mill, *Considerations on Representative Government*.
17  "Educational Attainment Statistics," Eurostat, 2021, https://ec.europa.eu/eurostat/statistics-explained/index.php?title=Educational_attainment_statistics.
18  See Stanley Fish, *Save the World on Your Own Time* (Oxford: Oxford University Press, 2008).
19  For example, consider a survey the LAS programmes in the Netherlands commissioned about their alumni. See Research Centre for Education and the Labour Market, *Liberal Arts & Sciences Programmes Alumni Survey Factsheet* (Maastricht: Maastricht University, 2017).

## References

Bok, Derek. *Beyond the Ivory Tower*. Cambridge, MA: Harvard University Press, 1982.
Brande, Luc van den. *Reaching out to EU Citizens—a New Opportunity*. Luxembourg: Publications Office of the European Union, 2017.
Dewey, John. *Democracy and Education: An Introduction to the Philosophy of Education*. London: Macmillan, 1923.
EHEA Ministerial Conference. "Statement of the Fifth Bologna Policy Forum." *News Release*, 2018.

"Educational Attainment Statistics." Eurostat, 2021. https://ec.europa.eu/eurostat/statistics-explained/index.php?title=Educational_attainment_statistics.

Feinberg, Walter. *Common Schools/Uncommon Identities: National Unity and Cultural Difference.* New Haven, CT: Yale University Press, 1998.

Fish, Stanley. *Save the World on Your Own Time.* Oxford: Oxford University Press, 2008.

Gutmann, Amy. *Democratic Education.* Princeton, NJ: Princeton University Press, 1999.

Halstead, Mark, and Mark Pike. *Citizenship and Moral Education: Values in Action.* London: Routledge, 2006.

Herheim, Rune, Tobias Werler, and Kjellrun Hiis Hauge, eds. *Lived Democracy in Education: Young Citizens' Democratic Lives in Kindergarten, School and Higher Education.* London: Routledge, 2021.

Jensen, Francis, and Amy Nutt. *The Teenage Brain: A Neuroscientist's Survival Guide to Raising Adolescents and Young Adults.* New York: HarperCollins, 2015.

Jubilee Centre for Character and Virtues. *A Framework for Character Education in Schools.* Birmingham: Jubilee Centre for Character and Virtues, University of Birmingham, 2017.

Jubilee Centre for Character and Virtues and Oxford Character Project. *Character Education in Universities: A Framework for Flourishing.* Birmingham: University of Birmingham, 2020.

Kiss, Elizabeth, and J. Peter Euben, eds. *Debating Moral Education: Rethinking the Role of the Modern University.* Durham, NC: Duke University Press, 2010.

Kristjánsson, Kristján. *Flourishing as the Aim of Education: A Neo-Aristotelian View.* London: Routledge, 2019.

Macedo, Stephen. *Diversity and Distrust: Civic Education in a Multicultural Democracy.* Cambridge, MA: Harvard University Press, 2009.

Nussbaum, Martha. *Cultivating Humanity: A Classical Defense of Reform in Liberal Education.* Cambridge, MA: Harvard University Press, 1998.

Nussbaum, Martha. *Not for Profit: Why Democracy Needs the Humanities.* Princeton, NJ: Princeton University Press, 2010.

Pike, Mark. "Christianity and Character Education: Faith in Core Values?" *Journal of Beliefs & Values* 31, no. 3 (2010): 311–21.

Research Centre for Education and the Labour Market. *Liberal Arts & Sciences Programmes Alumni Survey Factsheet.* Maastricht: Maastricht University, 2017.

White, Morgan. *Towards a Political Theory of the University: Public Reason, Democracy, and Higher Education.* London: Routledge, 2016.

# 4 Open-Mindedness and the Multidisciplinary Curriculum

*Q: What do you think a good democratic citizen is nowadays? What should you do or be able to do?*

*Doubt.*

Perhaps the civic virtue most central to having a genuine democratic conversation is open-mindedness. A democratic conversation is, by its very nature, a co-creative process in which participants consider different perspectives on social questions to arrive at shared conclusions. If one is not open-minded, that process cannot take place. The conversation serves no purpose if no one is willing to consider viewpoints other than their own or to change their mind. The political process becomes a series of performances that are only targeted at those who already agree and that do not advance anyone's understanding of the issues under consideration. Indeed, one of the main pathologies of modern democratic societies is that few citizens are ever willing to reconsider their opinions.

Even professional politicians see political debates more as an opportunity to present their preconceived solutions than to examine particular social issues and determine the best course of action. As a result, most political debates are fundamentally exercises in persuasion, rather than in deliberation. It is rare for parliamentarians to change their positions after listening to the contributions of political opponents. Indeed, if they do, it is considered a sign of inconsistency and weakness. This results in polarisation, makes compromise harder, and threatens the legitimacy of any measures that are enacted. Nor is a lack of open-mindedness limited to politics. In social discourse and the media, few people enter the conversation without firmly entrenched opinions, making conversations more like adversarial competitions than contributions to collective self-government. Here, too, this comes at a cost.

Open-mindedness is one of the most valuable things LAS students believe their education teaches them. It consistently came up in discussions.

DOI: 10.4324/9781003336594-4

As one student exclaimed when asked how their programme changed them as a person:

It's made me more open-minded, obviously.

When asked what they meant by open-minded, the response was:

Open-minded to different ideologies, beliefs, opinions, [and] engagement with different people.

One of the ways in which LAS programmes teach their students to be open-minded is through multidisciplinary curricula. It is by confronting students with different disciplinary perspectives that they come to understand that any way of looking at social issues is only a partial account of those issues and that different disciplines look at them in very different ways. Experience with different disciplines makes students aware that their initial views of matters are often incomplete and can be enriched by considering different viewpoints. This results in a certain humility and a willingness to engage with others in a conversation that is a joint exploration of the issues the community faces, as democracy requires, rather than a litigation with the sole goal of proving one was right all along. In short, as one student put it:

I think having an open mind can make you a better person. I think that's what liberal arts and sciences encourages, as well.

## Open-Mindedness

The idea that open-mindedness is an important virtue is a truism, and, as such, the concept is rarely defined with much precision. This makes it hard to see why it is a civic virtue and how it can be fostered. To remedy this, one might be inspired by a student who, in discussing the goals of liberal education, stressed the importance of escaping egocentrism:

[You need to leave] the egocentric [way] of viewing the universe. Which is so difficult. Because I have to [not] see myself as the centre of the universe. Looking at things from different angles, realising that the world is perhaps a lot more complex thing [than] you thought, that the very notion of truth can be questioned. [That there are], like, a lot of different perspectives.

Open-mindedness can be understood as an attitude of humility about what one knows and does not know. It is the belief that one's understanding of the world, and, in particular, one's understanding of social issues and the best way of dealing with them, is limited and partial. It requires one to recognise that one's preconceptions might be based on too little information, and that one's preferred solutions might very well be ineffective or have unforeseen consequences. This translates into a willingness to consider new insights, examine contradictory perspectives, and keep open the possibility of changing one's mind. As such, open-mindedness requires one to enter conversations without being wedded to a particular outcome; one certainly may have views to bring into the conversation, but these views should be offered as tentative and as subject to scrutiny and amendment or even rejection.

Many of the students interviewed believed open-mindedness to be highly valuable and key to being a good person:

> If we forget about the job market, career plans, and all of the other things that we talked about, I think being in this kind of education makes you more humble. It teaches you that your way is not the only way. . . . Unfortunately, many people miss out on that. I think we have an additional bonus. Not only is our career going to be, I hope, better in the future because we have this kind of education, but we're also going to be better people.

Open-mindedness stands opposed to closed-mindedness, which is the unshakable belief that one has all the relevant information and that one's understanding of the world corresponds to the way things actually are. Other views are simply wrong, and one could not ever imagine changing one's mind about important matters. When closed-minded people enter into a conversation, they do so with a preconceived notion of the outcome they wish to reach, and they aim to get others to see that they were right all along. Students found this kind of attitude deeply disconcerting. While most students, considering themselves open-minded, were reluctant to judge certain behaviours and attitudes as antithetical to liberal education, several remarked that they had observed fellow students get overly committed to certain ideas and come to take them to be infallible:

> It's somehow tricky but you are taught some ideas, right, in this programme or this method of education, and some people take these ideas too far and too seriously. [These people think] that they are ideas that no one can refute, and they are the ultimate truth. I think this is a pitfall or something bad people do.

## Open-Mindedness as a Democratic Virtue

Open-mindedness can seem like a rather wishy-washy concept, as if one should not have definite convictions or seek to convince others of one's point of view. Some have mocked it, warning that, if you open your mind too much, your brain will fall out. While open-mindedness certainly has its limits and needs to be balanced out by other virtues, such as the independence of thought that will be discussed in Chapter 5 and the sense of self considered in Chapter 6, it nevertheless is an important democratic virtue. A genuinely democratic conversation cannot get off the ground without it for several reasons.

Firstly, recall that democracy is, in part, based on the ideal of equal intrinsic worth. Citizens in a democracy regard each other as equals and seek to treat each other with equal respect. There is significant discussion about what exactly this requires, but one might argue that one thing equality demands, in the context of a democratic conversation, is being open to the input of fellow citizens. For if there is nothing a fellow citizen can say that will make one reconsider one's convictions, one is, in a way, denying that this person's perspective matters:

> Becoming a good citizen in a democratic society, I think it is about seeing all those different parts and not just saying, "Black and white, this is what I'm thinking. You are wrong when you don't think that."

One might even say that in refusing to consider other people's perspectives, one not only denies that their opinions matter but also that they matter as people. To the closed-minded, fellow citizens are not sources of opinions and insight that are, at least prima facie, worth investigating, if for no other reason than that they are held by fellow citizens. Engaging in a conversation with someone without allowing the possibility that anything they might say could have the slightest impact on one's thinking is to deny them equal status and is undemocratic for that reason. Rather, in a conversation of equals, one listens with interest to what others have to say, and one does so on the understanding that their contributions can influence one's ultimate conclusion. That is why being willing to change one's mind is something to be applauded:

> I also really respect people who change so much of their attitudes.

Secondly, there are epistemic advantages to open-mindedness that matter in the context of the democratic process. In a democratic conversation, each participant's perspective and experience can be considered a valuable resource, at least potentially; anyone might have an insight that reveals something important or falsifies a widely held assumption. However, these resources remain untapped if many people are closed-minded. It is only if individual participants in the conversation are willing to truly listen to what others have to say that the total wisdom of all participants can be used to come to meaningful conclusions. As discussed in Chapter 2, one of the reasons why democracy is a desirable political system is that it draws on the wisdom of the citizenry and tends to produce good outcomes because of this. But to do this well, people must consider the insights of their fellow citizens:

> I think being an academic, or researcher, or a person in general, you have to be quite humble to be able to solve difficult things because it's going to require more than what you can bring to the table anyway.

In this way, one of the great benefits of open-mindedness is that it preserves the character of democratic conversations. What makes this kind of conversation different from adversarial conversations is that one is concerned with achieving the optimal outcome for society as a whole, rather than getting what one wants at the expense of others. But there is always a danger that citizens will retreat into their own particular communities, and only argue from their own perspectives:

> I feel like [in] society nowadays, the big problem is that there is no cross-communication. Everyone is in this little societal bubble. . . . There's a lot of them. Everyone has different groupings of those [bubbles], "I'm a vegan." or, "I'm an environmental activist." or, "I'm right or left." But there's very little fluidity. So, I feel like, by doing liberal arts and refusing, in an academic setting, to already participate in those, I don't know how to say, [this] boxing up, then your brain is trained in a slightly different way, that would then maybe affect your way of looking at things [in ways] that influence democracy or [you] being a good person. Maybe you might be a bit more empathetic, or not see things as black and white.

Open-minded citizens, who are always willing to consider other perspectives, are much more likely to keep the goal of a democratic conversation in mind, as they are always engaging with others. This engagement reminds them that others' interests should also be considered.

Of course, one cannot legislate for open-mindedness, as it concerns an internal attitude. Nor can one force individuals to be open-minded towards others; one can never know if one's interlocutor is truly open-minded or is merely pretending to listen. Perhaps, in a free society, individuals even have a right to be closed-minded. And there are important discussions to be had concerning whether all perspectives should be included, including those that themselves deny the value of other perspectives. However, none of this means that it would not be beneficial to the democratic process if more people were more open-minded in fulfilling their role as citizens.

## Teaching Open-Mindedness through the Multidisciplinary Curriculum

Students in LAS programmes believe that their education helps them develop open-mindedness. When asked to explain what aspects of their programmes contributed to this, they pointed to several factors. Firstly, they believe that the diverse student populations that characterise many LAS programmes, in contrast to secondary school, contribute to a sense of open-mindedness. The idea seems to be that meeting people from different backgrounds makes one aware of the existence of the different perspectives that others may have. As one student pointed out when asked how studying LAS had made them more open-minded:

> I went to an all-boys private school, where a lot of people were from the same background. Now, it's a very different environment. I'm meeting all these people from different cultures. That's made me view things from this open-minded perspective. I [don't] mean open-minded in terms of social issues, I was always kind of that. But open-minded in terms of meeting new people, engaging with people that I wouldn't typically engage with, making friends with people from all over the world. That's the type of open-minded that [studying LAS] has made me.

Coming into contact with students from different backgrounds can make one aware that they have different perspectives, and if one can become friends with them, this might make one appreciate the value of their perspectives. This might generalise to an awareness that there are other perspectives out there that might also be valuable, resulting in an openness to other ways of looking at the world that one takes with one as one goes through life.

However, the feature of liberal education that students mentioned most often in reflecting on how their education fostered open-mindedness was the multidisciplinary nature of the curriculum. LAS programmes typically require students to study a diverse range of academic disciplines as part of the core curriculum and in their areas of focus. By studying a range of academic disciplines, students learn that these disciplines are mere representations of the world, and inherently present a partial interpretation of it. As one student remarked on their curriculum of sociology, philosophy, and religion courses:

> It's taught me how to look at how the world is presented to you and question that, because a presentation of the world is a presentation of the world. It's not a direct representation of how the world really is, and we've been taught to see it exactly as that, one way of looking at it.

Experience of multiple disciplines, students argued, made them much more open to the value of other perspectives than those who studied mono-disciplinary programmes. They worried that because students in those programmes are only taught one way of looking at the world, they might start to believe that this is indeed the way the world is:

> You have difficulty at times when talking to another student who is in a disciplinary programme and to explain your programme, and they don't understand the differences, the experience [of studying] different disciplines, often because they have been taught a specific view and that's it. I guess it isn't really narrow-minded. It's a very natural thing that they have. That kind of lack of experience, this causes them to be a bit more closed-minded.

Some students felt that there is a real danger that those who study only one discipline might take it as the only valid way of understanding the world. This may make them inclined to discount other perspectives and become unwilling to consider other views:

> People are predisposed to some ideas they like, and they adapt, and then they see more similar ideas here, and they say, "Okay, this is the ultimate truth then." and they become more opinionated and less critical.

In contrast to mono-disciplinary programmes, LAS students argued that liberal education makes one much more aware of the notion that different disciplines were created to make the world manageable by reducing its complexity and focusing on certain aspects of it but ignoring others. Disciplines are valuable tools for understanding parts of the world, but they cannot do justice to the world as a whole. Studying multiple disciplines is beneficial, one student said:

> because I think it's more true to the way the world really is. Not just like the career world we enter, but the nature of the world is that everything

flows together, and these disciplines are things we've [invented] to make order from chaos. Perhaps we can . . . go beyond these tools, to look at it all together as much as we can manage.

Interestingly enough, it was not only the multidisciplinary curriculum that helped students appreciate the value of other perspectives. Students also reported learning greater respect for other disciplines from interacting socially with fellow students who studied different disciplines than they did. As one student observed about taking classes with students who had taken different courses beforehand:

Quite often, various disciplines of science, they compete. There is sometimes even some contempt for other disciplines. I don't know, other scientists don't like mathematics and so on. I think that when you meet at the same faculty, in the same class, when you meet people who do completely different stuff, I think it teaches you some respect for the branches that maybe previously you didn't have so much respect for, but when you discuss it with these people you see that it's also science and that it is also valuable, that it makes sense.

Indeed, by not only taking the same classes together with students with a range of disciplinary interests but also by working on shared projects with them, students saw how different disciplines could contribute to a richer understanding of the issues under consideration and to better solutions:

through engagement with all the students that do completely different things. Here I've got so many peer students who major in sciences and engineering, that's completely different from what I'm doing. Then we're doing a group project and they're talking about things that I would've never thought of: "We could maybe incorporate this into our project." I thought, "Yes, sounds interesting. I've never thought about that, I don't even know what that is." I think that's definitely what you learn, and they try to explain it to you, and you explain your viewpoint on that to them, and you, together, come to a certain middle ground where you can incorporate all those different things.

Of course, there are downsides to the pursuit of open-mindedness. One issue that some students remarked on is how being open to other perspectives makes it hard to formulate an opinion on any given issue. If one is always seeking other perspectives and always questioning one's preconceptions, every opinion becomes tentative and subject to revision. This can be disorienting and makes it hard to participate in conversations, even if one recognises the value of open-mindedness. Disorientation is the price one must pay for learning how to be open-minded, but that does not diminish its value:

> Also, what I would say . . . is that, before I came to the liberal arts and sciences [programme], I had very, very many opinions and views on what I thought to be right and wrong. Now after two years, I rarely have any opinions on anything, I feel because I just question everything. That makes me sometimes feel lost because it is easier, and it feels more stable to have opinions. Now when I discuss politics with friends from years ago, and they know me as the one who's very opinionated, and now I'm just saying, "Well, I cannot make any statements [about] it because I don't have an opinion." That doesn't feel very good, but I think it's still a process and I think it will give me a very valuable result in the end.

# 5 Independence of Thought and Active Pedagogy

*[A good citizen is] also somebody who knows when to call bullshit. Again, taking care of your own safety, being strategic, pick your battles, fine, but you need to also call bullshit. I think that's a good citizen.*

While citizens in a democratic society must be open to different perspectives and ways of thinking about social problems, this does not mean that they should believe everything they are told without question. Rather, they should be sceptical of how political issues and suggested solutions are presented to them, subjecting information to critical scrutiny to come to an independent assessment of its merits. If they do not do this, they are not really participating in self-rule, but rather slavishly following the judgment of others. This opens citizens up to manipulation by not only their own governments but also by powerful interests in society or from abroad.

These are not just theoretical possibilities. The rise of fake news, i.e., the deliberate fabrication of news stories to influence people's perceptions of current affairs, sometimes promoted by foreign governments or interest groups, threatens to mislead citizens and undermine their ability to fulfil their democratic role. This is aggravated by social media, which selectively present users with information based on previous online activity, making it less likely that they will see information that offers an alternative view of the issues. These are not new problems. There is a long history of governments or press barons using the media to selectively inform the population or even to manipulate the people through propaganda.

In a healthy democracy, citizens are able to critically examine the information they are presented with to determine whether it is trustworthy and to come to their own, independent judgments. LAS students are firmly convinced that their education teaches them this kind of independence of thought. Independent thinking consistently came up in discussing what

DOI: 10.4324/9781003336594-5

skills students developed during their education. For example, one student, in considering the goals of a LAS programme, observed:

> I think that what a liberal arts and sciences programme definitely does is to [teach you to] think critically, to be critical of what is going on.

In reflecting on how their programmes taught them independence of thought, students argued that one of the key features was the active, student-centred pedagogy that LAS programmes typically employ. By creating a classroom environment in which students actively discuss and evaluate the material they are studying, they learn how to question information and arguments. This fosters a critical culture, which creates a habit of mind that students expect to take with them after they graduate:

> I think allowing students to have discussions, and allowing students to read radically different opinions, and talk about them, and ask [questions], and be critical of the standard opinion, that changes you. You will question everything after that. After doing that for a bit, nothing is normal anymore.[1]

## Independence of Thought

The basic idea behind independence of thought is that when one is presented with facts, analyses of social issues, and solutions to those issues, one does not accept them as true without carefully assessing them. One must scrutinise the information one is presented with and scrupulously test it to determine if it can withstand that scrutiny and what weight one should attach to it. One might do so in all kinds of ways. For example, one might check whether the information contains internal contradictions, whether it accords well with other information that one is aware of, whether it was gathered in a rigorous fashion, whether the source is credible, or whether someone might have an inappropriate interest in presenting it. Only by asking these questions can one truly evaluate the information and decide whether or not to accept it. The opposite of independence of thought might be called dependence of thought, which refers to accepting information uncritically, without going through the process of systematically scrutinising it.

It is important to distinguish between independence of thought and critical thinking. Both concepts are obviously related. However, critical thinking, as it is used in discussions about education, is much wider. It is often used as synonymous with all rational, evidence-based, or structured thinking. Independence of thought, as it is used here, is more specific, referring to a critical, i.e., sceptical, attitude to claims that are advanced in order to make one's own judgment about them. This is part of critical thinking, but, for present purposes, it is helpful to focus on the narrower concept because of its importance to the democratic process.[2]

While one can apply critical scrutiny to all kinds of information, arguments, and proposed courses of action, independence of thought should certainly be applied to generally accepted assumptions in society. In every society, there is conventional wisdom, i.e., "ideas which are esteemed at any time for their acceptability."[3] Some of these ideas might be supported by excellent reasons, but others might be highly flawed and only credible because many people in society believe them. Independent thinkers dare to question such ideas, asking whether they are indeed worth accepting, while dependent thinkers take these ideas for granted. As such, independent thinkers are always willing to challenge the status quo and are sceptical of official truths propagated by those in power. As one student observed in considering the idea that liberal education should educate students for citizenship:

> It's really dangerous, not for the students, but for the system.
> Q: How so? What's the danger?
> That you have critical minds and that these challenge the status quo, the accepted wisdom. But I think it's great.

Independence of thought requires both the skills and knowledge to ask and answer questions about the information one is presented with, but it also requires the habit of mind to do so in daily life. This must become second nature. It is one thing to scrutinise information in the context of an academic seminar, in which this is explicitly expected, but quite another to do so when one is watching the news or having a conversation with a fellow citizen. However, independence of thought is most important when it is hardest; it is in those moments that one is most likely to accept information without asking critical questions.

There is a complex but symbiotic relationship between independence of thought and open-mindedness. The latter is all about being willing to consider new information without prejudice, to give ideas a chance, even if they might seem strange or counterintuitive. The former concerns testing them rigorously and ultimately accepting or rejecting them. Too much open-mindedness is problematic because it might lead one to accept information and ideas uncritically. But too much independence of thought might result in one dismissing new insights too quickly and not considering the valuable aspects of other perspectives. Hence, the two must be balanced; one must always consider the possibility that there is great value in other ways of looking at matters, but one should always check whether this is, in fact, the case. This is not always easy. It requires one to have a split attitude: on the one hand, always being curious, but on the other, constantly looking for reasons to discard new insights. Only by walking this line can one make sure that one does not miss anything important.

## Independence of Thought as a Democratic Virtue

One reason why independence of thought is a crucial civic virtue is that it is a necessary condition of freedom. The ideal of collective self-governance starts from the assumption that individuals are capable of thinking for themselves. It is because they have that capacity that individuals can participate in the governing process as free citizens. If one is ready to uncritically accept whatever one is told, one is not really an active participant in the process but rather a means through which others shape decisions. This makes one unfree in a fundamental sense. To make the same point differently, those who participate in a democratic conversation by simply repeating what others have said are not participating. Of course, that does not mean that one cannot agree with others or support arguments that have already been made. However, what is crucial is that one does so independently, i.e., after having subjected positions to critical scrutiny and having formed one's own opinion about them. It is in doing so that one makes those positions one's own and thereby frees oneself from being someone else's agent:

> A free person is something that we can only become if we have enough knowledge. Because we have the freedom of thinking and the freedom of making good decisions, I think, if we are able to think critically.

This may be an abstract point about the nature of freedom, but it has concrete implications. For citizens who are dependent thinkers can easily be controlled, which poses a threat to democracy. Imagine a situation in which foreign powers or rich individuals manage to deceive an uncritical group of citizens into accepting arguments and solutions that benefit these manipulators, perhaps by controlling the media or planting fake news. A majority of citizens blindly believe what they are told and support the solutions, which are then enacted. This decision can hardly be said to be the product of democratic self-governance. It is the product of manipulation, and the citizens are as unfree as they would be in any dictatorship. Indeed, matters might be worse than in a dictatorship, because in a dictatorship at least it is clear that the people are not free, whereas in this situation, the process might appear impeccably democratic.

Moreover, independence of thought is important in holding the government of the day to account. In a representative democracy, one of the key functions of citizens is to determine whether those in power are doing an acceptable job or whether they should be removed. To do so, citizens must be able to assess the government's actions. This requires them to critically scrutinise information that is presented by the government and the media about its activities. Those in power will always present their work as a great success, but if citizens simply accept this without thinking for themselves, they can easily be misled into supporting governments that are not delivering for their citizens. If this happens, the rulers effectively control whether or not they remain in power. In this way, too, democratic governance lives and dies by citizens being able to think independently. As one student answered when asked what a good citizen is:

> I think most importantly, he can think critically. Because if you can't think critically, you're just at a stage where everything that is told to you, you just believe. I don't think that's healthy for a democracy.

Independence of thought is also important to ensure the epistemic value of democratic conversations. Recall that one of the advantages of such a conversation is that it tends to lead to good decisions, in part because it aggregates the wisdom of large numbers of citizens. However, for this argument about the aggregation of wisdom to work, it is important that citizens think independently and form their own opinions, based on an individual assessment of all the relevant facts. If some citizens do not think independently, then they do not really contribute their wisdom, they simply amplify the voices of others. This effectively reduces the number of judgments that are aggregated, making the conclusions less robust. After all, the idea of the jury theorem is that if a large group of people converges on a decision, it is likely to be a good decision. However, if many people simply copy the assessments of a few, then the group of assessors becomes much smaller. Moreover, if citizens slavishly follow the judgements of others, they might end up supporting policies that are not in their self-interest, but rather in the interests of those who they follow, as was noted by one student who explained:

> Some people, [I] think they really are biased in a way, because they go with what the majority thinks is good. But then they don't really come to see what is good for them individually or for others individually.

Rousseau was concerned about this issue when he noted the dangers presented by political parties and other social groups.[4] He argued that if members blindly follow the instructions of the parties they are affiliated with, the only people who are actually engaged in the political process are the leaders of these parties. This turns democracy from rule of the many into rule of the few. There is also a danger that the leaders will start to prioritise the interest of their groups over the interest of the community as a whole. After all, clearly defined social groups tend to develop group consciousness. Leaders feel responsible for their members and seek to get the best deal for them, even at the expense of others. However, if this happens, politics can become a competition of factional interests, rather than a collective search for the best outcome for society as a whole. Such competition threatens democratic conversations, turning them into either persuasion games or negotiations. As a result, democracy becomes rule not only by the few, but also for the few, and the results do not have the legitimacy that is generated by a collective search for the common good.

To be sure, the importance of independence of thought does not require every citizen to re-invent the wheel. Very few individuals have either the time, the ability, or the inclination to do independent research on political issues. It is entirely proper for them to base their judgments on information they get through the media, or from experts, interest groups, and the government. However, they do have a responsibility to evaluate this information critically and not to take what they are told for granted, so that they can independently make up their own minds about the issues. Only if they do so can they fulfil their role as democratic citizens well.

## Teaching Independence of Thought Through Active Pedagogy

When asked how liberal education promotes independence of thought, LAS students pointed to a number of its characteristics. The multidisciplinary nature of the curriculum, which played an important role in helping students develop an open mind by exposing them to different perspectives on issues, also made them sceptical towards authoritative claims. Students in LAS programmes constantly see that different disciplines look at issues differently, and so they are open to the possibility that information and arguments that they are presented with might not be the full story. Being used to considering different perspectives, it becomes second nature to ask what can be said against a particular line of thought. As one student pointed out when asked how liberal education taught a sceptical attitude:

> Just by giving you insight into so many subjects that one is careful [about] too authoritative statements of people that say, "I have figured it out now. After thousands of years, guys. Listen to me. I got it." You can say, "Yes. Maybe you've got something, but let's be careful. Maybe your idea is not completely refined yet. Let's talk about it."[5]

However, the main way in which students felt LAS education teaches independence of thought was by using highly active and student-centred pedagogies. In many universities, most teaching happens through lectures given to large audiences, in which highly qualified professors explain the subject-specific material students are expected to master. These lectures might be complemented by smaller meetings, in which students are allowed to ask clarificatory questions to ensure they have understood the content of the lectures. Exams then test this understanding by asking students to answer questions about the material, or perhaps requiring them to apply it to concrete cases. The fundamental goal is to transmit the understanding the teachers have to the students and to assess to what extent they have internalised it. By contrast, LAS programmes typically use small-scale pedagogies in which students take a much more active role; rather than being passive receptacles of knowledge that are filled by authorities on the subject, the classroom centres around student-led discussion. Different programmes facilitate this discussion in different ways, whether through problem-based learning or small classes and seminars. However, what is key is that the LAS model of education encourages students not merely to internalise facts, theories, and concepts but invites them to question these. As one student remarked:

> We also have to evaluate things. We have to evaluate theories, evaluate articles. It's not just, "Read it, okay, this must be it then. This must be the answer." That's how we were taught to be critical, to constantly think about what we're receiving and think about what we're reading before we accept that as being the answer.

One of the things that LAS programmes do to encourage this kind of critical attitude is to carefully select what literature students are expected to read before class. In many cases, courses focus on primary literature, rather than employing secondary literature or textbooks that offer definite interpretations of scholarly concepts and theories. Students are presented with original texts written by renowned scholars and are left to form their own opinions of them. This requires in-depth study and careful analysis of the material:

> Well, independence of thought, I think, like I said, it [requires] very close reading, very close reading. So, we don't really get, like, secondary texts. Like, . . . there really isn't that much to form an opinion off of, other than like a source text . . . , which I think fosters, like, being able to be critical [and have] independence of thought.

Moreover, some students explained that they were often asked to read texts that reached opposite conclusions or to apply theories to particular cases.

Both of these strategies serve to tease out the implications of what students have read and invite a critical assessment of the material:

> In most of my classes, we have different literatures and we compared them, and we could see the contradictions that they have and [distil] the vital points that they make. . . . Then, most of the time we would also apply this to real-life cases, so that you see, how does the theory then play out in the real world, and then we see a lot of the things that you take for granted. When you question them, then you might see the different perspectives to it.[6]

In this type of pedagogy, teachers have a distinctive role. They are not fonts of knowledge or authorities to please. For if they take that role and simply impart their knowledge to their students, these students might very well take that knowledge as absolutely true. After all, the teachers are the experts, and students are there to learn from them. Moreover, if students are assessed through exams that test whether they can reproduce what their teachers have told them, students will have an incentive to focus on internalising the perspectives of their teachers. But in LAS programmes, teachers aim to stimulate students to question the information they have received, trying to get them to consider possible objections to it. One student explained that teachers really seek to provoke students, arguing:

> There are many courses where the professor plays the devil's advocate and always questions whatever you do. You say something and then the lecturer [goes] . . . like, "Have you thought about this one?" With that, you get the personal skills of questioning yourself in certain situations.

Students felt that studying LAS made them better able to think independently than a more traditional programme would have. The active classroom taught them a questioning attitude that they would not have learned by merely attending lectures and internalising assigned material. As they progressed through their studies, they developed a critical habit of mind. As one student observed:

> I think especially now that I'm in my third year, and I sit in a class, half of our class is debating, "Well, I wouldn't agree with that." If we read a paper, then we're like, "Oh, but this is an awful paper." Whereas I think if I had [done] a different degree [programme], I might have been more inclined to just take it at face value. I think the ability to criticise and think for yourself is something I've gained here.

This insight was seconded by a recent graduate of a LAS programme who was currently studying in a more traditional graduate programme in psychology, and who was hence able to compare the two. The student reflected on the difference as follows:

> I feel like there are very few truths in what we've learned so far. It's really, I would say . . . , we've learned methods and we've learned about certain, maybe schools of thought. Then it's more this thing of, "Look, here's an argument and make of it what you will, agree, disagree. Find your own arguments for it." Yes, I would say that that's been a very central part of my previous education and something that I'm certainly missing now with psychology, where it's like, "Here, this is a fact. Learn it by heart."

This independence of thought, and especially the constant questioning that comes with it, was occasionally experienced as a burden. Questioning accepted wisdom can make one unpopular with those who are less critically inclined, as many students recognised. One said:

> This might sound a little bit cliché, but I think having a really critical tendency towards things that are generally accepted has caused me a lot of trouble at family gatherings, or with families, or friends.

However, at the same time, independence of thought can be liberating. For when one questions what one is told, one also realises that assumptions that appear to be self-evident truths are often not as fixed as they appear but are matters of social convention or of one's own ignorance. In questioning them, one realises this, and these truths become less constraining, making one a freer person:

> Well, for me, with the experience that everything is criticised and questioned . . . , you're really pushed to see all the boundaries that are set upon you by society or your personality, or psychology, or whatever. That might be a hard experience to acknowledge, or to recognise, all these boundaries. Once you recognise them, you can overcome them, and maybe see how you can free yourself from them, and distance yourself from [them].

## Notes

1 Also appears in Teun Dekker, "Teaching Critical Thinking through Engagement with Multiplicity," *Thinking Skills and Creativity* 37 (2020).
2 For a discussion of how LAS students understand the wider and more general concept of critical thinking and how their education helps them develop the

ability to think critically, see Teun Dekker, "Teaching Critical Thinking through Engagement with Multiplicity," Thinking Skills and Creativity 37 (2020). However, since critical thinking and independence of thought are related, three quotes from that paper also appear here.
3  John Kenneth Galbraith, *The Affluent Society* (Boston, MA: Houghton Mifflin Harcourt, 1998), 8.
4  Jean-Jacques Rousseau, *Of the Social Contract*, book 2, chapter 3.
5  Also appears in Dekker, "Teaching Critical Thinking through Engagement with Multiplicity."
6  Ibid.

## References

Dekker, Teun. "Teaching Critical Thinking through Engagement with Multiplicity." *Thinking Skills and Creativity* 37 (2020): 100701.
Galbraith, John Kenneth. *The Affluent Society*. Boston, MA: Houghton Mifflin Harcourt, 1998.

# 6  The Sense of Self and Freedom of Choice

*Personality is more. Maybe by personality, I mean getting into a relationship with yourself, and then being able to find a place in society from where you can add, and also question this place.*

In higher education, students learn about many things, whether it be academic theories and concepts, facts about the world, scientific disciplines, or research methods. However, they also learn about themselves; they develop a sense of their own identities as individuals and the roles they want to play in society. This is hugely important for them generally, but it is also an essential civic virtue in a democracy. Only those who have a sense of who they are and what their beliefs are can provide meaningful input into democratic conversations.

Few university programmes systematically support students in developing this sense of self. It is rarely considered an explicit goal of higher education, and students are often left to their own devices in this process. However, LAS students often feel that their education encourages them to think about who they are:

> It's very introspective to be here, I think. That's incredibly important. Maybe that's the most important thing that we learned here. We learn who we are. I think you can't really put that, as I said, on a CV. [But] that's what we are encouraged to do here.

Giving students freedom of choice is central to how LAS programmes foster a sense of self. By requiring students to make their own choices about their education – for example, by allowing them to select their own topics for papers or by giving them the freedom to design their curricula – these programmes encourage students to develop a personal narrative, and this forces them to answer questions about their positions in current debates,

DOI: 10.4324/9781003336594-6

the issues they are interested in, and their strengths and weaknesses. In programmes with pre-defined and inflexible curricula, students never have to question what they are studying or how the various parts of their education relate because the answers have already been determined by the programme. One student explained this well when considering how liberal education can help one become a free person:

> Okay, so I think that liberal arts is not an education that is set out for you. You really need to make this education yours. Because of this, you . . . constantly need to defend your choices to yourself, really think about that, and see how they all fit, and you create this narrative in your head of what it is that you're doing. . . .
>
> Q: If you had studied economics, would you now have been less free?
>
> Well, in a sense, yes. Because I think that part of the marvellous thing about this is that, yes, you really get to not be afraid of the challenge and of . . . being confronted with uncertainty, and not knowing, because this is a situation in which all the different things that you choose in your curriculum are not necessarily entirely related, or they're not meant to be related, like, built up as a follow-up course. You need to make all of these bridges and connections yourself. This is training and I don't think a lot of other programmes do that, precisely because they've been set up as, "This is a course that you have [to take]." In a way, this allows you to really think about what you want to do as well, and so you go into the world with more of a give and take outlook, I guess, where you're like, "Okay, I would like my life to look like this."

## The Sense of Self

Young people trying to find themselves is one of the great clichés about growing up. It conjures up images of teenagers trekking through India or working on organic farms in the hope of discovering who they truly are. Like most clichés, the concept is vague; it is rarely made clear what exactly it means to find yourself or, indeed, what it would mean *not* to find yourself. Perhaps this vagueness adds to universities' reluctance to explicitly make developing a sense of self part of their educational mission. However, when one considers how having a clearly defined identity could be beneficial for citizens in a democratic society, it becomes possible to specify three central aspects of the sense of self, namely, one's perspectives on issues of concern, one's preferences, and one's strengths and weaknesses.

Firstly, having a sense of self means having a considered opinion about various problems and controversies, i.e., having an individual perspective on them. In a way, this is a synthesis of open-mindedness and independence of thought. After having examined various possible ways of looking at issues and having interrogated them independently, one must decide how to weigh the various arguments and which perspective one finds most persuasive. For example, one might have had occasion to consider various ways of limiting the effects of climate change. After being open to different options and carefully scrutinising them, one must decide which ones are, all things considered, the best options. As one student put it in reflecting on how their education enabled them to deal with different ways of looking at things:

> Just taking your responsibility to say, "This is what I stand for." Eventually, after you've come to the point where it's like, "This is what I think."

Secondly, a sense of self requires understanding what one likes and what one wants. In part, it is about knowing what one finds interesting and exciting but also what one wishes to do with one's life, what one's ambitions and desires are, and what one regards as beneficial. Inspired by the philosopher Ronald Dworkin, these might be called one's preferences, and they are fundamentally self-regarding, in contrast to one's beliefs about the world, which are more external.[1] Obviously, the two are related, in that what one thinks about various issues is shaped by one's ideas about what is valuable and vice versa, but there is nevertheless a worthwhile distinction to be made between the two. After all, one might agree with someone about the best way of tackling climate change but disagree about whether philosophy is more interesting than sociology, or whether one should live a life of action or contemplation. Coming to an understanding of one's preferences is an important part of LAS education, as one student explained in discussing how their education had shaped them:

> It maybe made me just more open to exploring, but also [able to say more clearly], "I enjoy this, and I don't enjoy this." or, "This is my preference."

Thirdly, a sense of self involves knowing one's strengths and weaknesses and what one is capable of. This, too, is self-regarding knowledge, but it is different from knowing one's preferences. Rather, it concerns one's personal resources. These are related to one's preferences in many cases; those who are good at statistics might decide that they want to use those abilities in their future careers. However, preferences and personal resources are also independent, as one might have ambitions in areas where one is less talented. This understanding of one's abilities, and in some sense one's character, was aptly described by a student who reflected on the most important thing their education had taught them:

> I've learned a lot about what makes me tick, what hurts me . . . I have learned so much more about my position in the world, and what I can do with it, and how I can mould it a little bit, and how I can support myself to become better at learning, and just tweaking and changing. I think that's really important.

## The Sense of Self as a Democratic Virtue

Having a sense of self is an important democratic virtue because it is required to participate well in a democratic conversation. Of course, the importance of a sense of self goes beyond the democratic process. If a person has little awareness of what they believe or the sort of person they are, they are unlikely to be able to make satisfying choices for themselves in any domain of life or operate effectively in any context. But in collective self-governance, a sense of self is particularly significant.

Consider the importance of having an individual perspective on issues, of knowing what one believes. The idea of a democratic conversation is that everybody contributes their perspectives to discussions about issues of shared concern. By exchanging arguments and compromising, participants reach an agreement. If all goes well, this agreement will have a certain degree of legitimacy and is likely to be a good decision because everyone has contributed their perspectives. All of this is premised on participants having a particular viewpoint. They must have come to a considered opinion about the issues, and they must be able to explain why they have this opinion, as well as how they arrived at it. Those who do not have a particular perspective simply cannot participate. Of course, an individual perspective can be developed gradually, as one participates in the democratic process, by informing oneself, listening to arguments, and considering what to vote for. In many ways, participation and perspective are symbiotic in that what one believes shapes how one participates, but one's participation also shapes one's beliefs. However, one must enter the conversation with a particular perspective that is based on one's prior engagement with the topic under discussion. As one student reflected in considering how to make good judgments:

> If you've taken part in the liberal arts philosophy, then you've thought about who you are as a person, who you are in the context of what

you've studied, who you are in the context of everything you've seen, you make links between your different areas of life. Through that, you build your own idea and your own perception of who you are, and I think that's very much what's needed for citizenship.

Similarly, having a conception of one's preferences is also important if one wishes to be a good citizen. After all, a democratic conversation is supposed to consider the preferences of all citizens; in deciding what is to be done, participants in such conversations must consider the effects of measures on different individuals as they search for the best overall outcome. However, every individual's good is a part of the common good. This means that one must be able to determine what outcomes one would prefer, and to do so, one must have a clear conception of one's preferences and whether one would benefit from a particular measure. Those who do not know what they want out of life cannot judge this. Nor can they present their positions to others or explain how they would be impacted by collective decisions. As a result, their concerns risk being overlooked, or they may support solutions that are not actually in their self-interest. If this happens, democratic conversations no longer serve those individuals and the process can no longer be considered rule in the interest of all. As the same student observed in reflecting on how studying liberal arts helped them develop their voice as a citizen:

> You have to have a good awareness of what matters to you before you can then apply that and take action on that.

Lastly, citizens must have a clear sense of their strengths and weaknesses to participate in democratic conversations. This is required to understand how they can contribute to the conversation and to society in general. Inevitably, not all citizens will be able to contribute to self-governance in the same way given their specific talents. Some might have the ability to engage underrepresented groups, while others might have a high level of technocratic knowledge. Moreover, individuals can contribute to society in different ways. Some may do so by running for office, while others might do so by being active in social movements. For everyone to give what they are best able to contribute, they must understand their strengths and weaknesses. Here, too, there is a relationship with other aspects of the sense of self. If you know you are good at organising marginalised groups, you are likely to have the desire to do so, though you might also not have this desire, despite having the talent. In any case, to be a good member of a self-governing society, one must understand how one can contribute to that community. If one lacks this awareness, one is not going to be able to direct one's efforts appropriately. As a student reflected when considering what it means to be a good person in contemporary society:

> You can contextualise yourself in a community, you can think about all the different angles [from] which you as a person could contribute or maybe refuse to contribute. Having this knowledge and having to deal . . . with this knowledge, knowing that if you want to go for a certain career that you will only contribute to society in one way, but really harm it in another way, I think this is something that, for me at least, [is] the basis of being a good person.

## Teaching the Sense of Self Through Freedom of Choice

LAS programmes encourage students to develop a sense of self by giving them the freedom to design their own education. Rather than seeing students as passive consumers of a pre-made course of studies, LAS programmes expect their students to take an active role in shaping their education. By giving students control, they force them to reflect on the choices they must make, and this, in turn, helps students develop a sense of self. In other words, allowing students to shape their own education forces them to construct a coherent narrative of their studies, and in that process, they learn about who they are:

> I think that there are things that you can only learn about yourself if you have a choice. This is because of how hard it is to make certain choices and because of how you will then have to deal with the choices that you make. That doesn't necessarily come about if you have a set curriculum.

One important way in which LAS programmes allow students to shape their education is by using open forms of assessment. In these forms of assessment, students have the opportunity to select the topics or issues they wish to work on. For example, by asking students to write papers or give presentations after picking their own research questions or cases, and by asking them to formulate their own arguments, students experience the freedom to pursue what they find interesting. These forms of assessment are quite different from closed forms of assessment, such as traditional exams or assignments, in which teachers design the questions and students must provide the answers, and which mainly test students' ability to reproduce knowledge or apply theories to cases. Of course, many traditional programmes allow students to write papers and select their own topics, but they typically reserve this for the very end of the programme, whereas LAS programmes usually include these types of assignments from the very start.

Students experience the process of selecting questions and topics as difficult but rewarding. In making choices, they negotiate freedom, and in doing so, they must reflect on who they are and what they think about various issues. After all, one can only decide which topics to study in the light of what one finds interesting. Moreover, in studying the issues one has chosen, one is forced to consider different ways of looking at them and to come to one's own conclusions. One student explained the freedom they experienced when writing papers as follows:

> We have to ask the question in the paper for ourselves. It's okay, you are confronted with possibilities because freedom can sometimes be like suicide, [in] that you don't know what to do because you could do everything. That's when you sit in front of an empty Word document and come up with something, and [then] freedom is more real, like feeling what you want and what you think.

Interestingly, students often make such choices in the light of their work in other courses or for previous assignments, taking up similar themes or advancing complementary arguments. In this way, each paper or presentation is not just an isolated piece of work but is inspired by and contributes to a student's academic profile:

> Also, within classes, [we have to decide] how we're going to tailor the class to us. That might sound a bit strange, but which essay title you're going to pick . . . could tie into something you're doing in another class.

However, the most obvious way in which LAS programmes allow students to develop a sense of self is by giving them considerable freedom of choice in the courses they wish to take. Unlike traditional programmes, which largely consist of pre-determined modules and which reserve elective courses for the later years, LAS programmes allow students to select their courses of studies from a wide range of options. While students must meet a number of requirements, ensuring both breadth and sufficient specialisation, they enjoy a great deal of curricular freedom.

With great freedom comes great responsibility; those who may choose must choose wisely. Students are challenged to compose a coherent curriculum out of several different elements. To do so, they must articulate a story that explains how various courses relate to each other and how they form a coherent preparation for their future plans. This is a gradual process in which students make choices in the context of their reflections on the courses they have taken before.[2] While students may initially be somewhat casual in their choices, as they progress, they often become much more thoughtful about how their courses relate and how they contribute to their overall curricula. In this process, students develop a much clearer conception of what they are truly interested in. As one student pointed out, after observing that they initially chose courses somewhat unreflectively:

> I feel like now I'm very much aware [in] choosing modules, especially [in] trying to make my path and link things . . . and how things impact one another. So, I think about things more in terms of what will it bring me, how does it fit into my narrative, how does it all fit together? I feel like I think a lot more comprehensively about every single [one] of my decisions. I always add it to this little path of where I go.

One of the ways in which LAS programmes stimulate this kind of reflection is by insisting students justify their choices to academic advisors or personal tutors, typically in individual or group meetings, before choices are formalised. This requires them to articulate their rationales for the choices they are making. In doing so, they develop the vocabulary to describe their preferences and ambitions, and the confidence to act on them:

> I think you need to be able to confidently speak [about] these things, to be able to make a case for what you're studying in front of your peers, in front of your personal tutor. . . . I think all of those steps really push us to take initiative, but also to be proud of them and take ownership of that, rather than just let it all happen to us.

As this student indicates, it is not only the conversations with personal tutors and advisors that help students formulate a coherent narrative about their education but conversations with fellow students as well. Since all students in these programmes must go through this process, there is typically a lot of conversation among students about their course choices. This, too, gives students an opportunity to articulate their reasons for taking certain courses and to discuss how their curricula add up to something more than the sum of their parts:

> It is seeing other people going through the same thing and talking about it with them. If liberal education, if this reflection process would really be only a self-reflection, in the sense that you sit on your own, alone, and make notes about it, that would not help a lot. But as we do it together, it's very helpful.

This process of reflecting on one's curriculum and what it implies for one's future plans was often experienced as deeply frustrating. Inevitably, earlier plans and, with them, conceptions of one's identity are upended. There are moments when choices are questioned, or when the eventual goal of one's studies is, if only temporarily, forgotten. In considering how their education had changed them, one student said:

> I think that was a very, very difficult question for me in particular, studying with the [purpose of] understanding who I am. Because, I am now, for about half a year, in an absolute identity crisis. I don't understand myself anymore at all and I think LAS has contributed greatly to this crisis. It's very hard and stressful but then again, I see that it might be necessary in order to overcome some boundaries I had set before.

Students mentioned that navigating moments of crisis helped them come to terms with their strengths and weaknesses, and to discover important truths about their characters:

> It is under circumstances of stress that you are most yourself. I think that this liberal arts and sciences concept can really push people to moments of personal stress, or academic stress, or social stress. It really shapes people in one direction or another, which I think is good.

Perhaps because of all the effort and frustration students experienced in designing their curricula, they often ended up feeling quite proud of them. After all, their courses of studies were something they had invested considerable thought into, agonised over, and ultimately committed to:

> I designed this. This is my personal curriculum. No one else has this curriculum and I decided to do exactly this. There's no one telling me, "Oh, you should have taken this course or that one." No, I am the one who can now, at the end of my studies, say this.

Developing a sense of self, especially as it is required for democratic citizenship, is not restricted to formal education. Citizens develop this sense of self in many different ways, and it is a life-long process. Studying LAS can, however, contribute to this. It can give students some tentative idea of their opinions about issues, their preferences and abilities, and their characters. As such, giving students control over their education can go some way to helping them think about who they are and how they want to live, both individually and in society. That is a good start. As one student answered when asked about the most important thing their education had taught them:

> I really learned what I find important or how I am trying to live my life, even though I'm not fully sure where I'm exactly going after this. I know that I have certain ideals or principles, and just a general idea of how I want to treat the people around me. . . . The questioning and

asking yourself, or analysing yourself, helps you to just overcome some character flaws or character traits that are, I don't know, not really productive when you want to live among people.

## Notes

1  See Ronald Dworkin, "What Is Equality? Part 2: Equality of Resources," *Philosophy & Public Affairs* 10, no. 4 (1981).
2  See Teun Dekker, "The Value of Curricular Choice through Student Eyes," *The Curriculum Journal* 32, no. 2 (2021).

## References

Dekker, Teun. "The Value of Curricular Choice through Student Eyes." *The Curriculum Journal* 32, no. 2 (2021): 198–214.
Dworkin, Ronald. "What Is Equality? Part 2: Equality of Resources." *Philosophy & Public Affairs* 10, no. 4 (1981): 283–345.

# 7    The Sense of the Other and the International Classroom

*A good person is someone who tries to see beyond [their] own horizons. For example, [that] entails empathy, [that] entails that I do not only consider knowledge as being measured in, for example, numbers. It allows [me] to really see, who is that person, who am I talking to in this specific moment, and what is important to [them]. Because that's what we get taught [for] three years throughout this curriculum. There are so many different people, and they all want something different from this programme. This is why I think that makes you a good person, see[ing] who is there.*

In democratic conversations, people with different backgrounds, interests, and ideas come together to agree, as far as possible, on solutions to shared problems. Through the exchange of arguments and perspectives, they try to find a course of action that does justice to all concerned and serves the common good. To do so, one must understand one's fellow citizens. One must have some insight into their cultures and values, their perspectives on issues, as well as the circumstances from which they hail. This is required to judge how they will be affected by certain measures, but it is also essential to having a productive, democratic conversation with them. In short, collective self-governance requires a sense of the other.

Higher education provides a wonderful opportunity for young people to develop this sense of the other. In secondary school, during which most students live at home, they are much less likely to encounter people from very different backgrounds than at university. But a sense of the other does not spontaneously arise. An educational environment needs to be carefully designed to foster it. In part, this is a matter of ensuring that the student population itself is diverse, with students coming from different countries and backgrounds. However, this is necessary but not sufficient; in a lecture-based system of education, in which students simply attend presentations by professors, go home, memorise information, and regurgitate it during exams, it does not matter where the students come from. After all, students

DOI: 10.4324/9781003336594-7

do not interact with each other in any meaningful way, at least not in the context of their education, and so they are unlikely to gain an understanding of each other. Rather, the experience of students needs to be curated to ensure that they gain such an understanding. LAS programmes provide a helpful model of how this can be achieved. They are designed to be highly international communities, in which the curriculum, the methods of education, and the social environment work together to create what has been called an international classroom.[1]

Students from LAS programmes believe that studying in such an environment helps them cultivate a sense of the other, and they regard this as highly valuable. As one student explained when discussing which aspects of their education helped them gain an awareness of the perspectives of other people:

> Definitely being in contact with people from international backgrounds. Being in contact with other languages. Being in contact with people who are very different than I am. It made me more tolerant. It made me more open. It made me more relaxed in just being around difference. I think, unfortunately, many of us are confined to a space that doesn't have a lot of difference and a lot of variety before we get to university. If we dive straight in, just like I did here, and everybody else that comes here does as well, I think that's [an] incredibly valuable experience. It's so interesting. It's so much fun to be around this kind of diversity.

## The Sense of the Other

At its most basic level, having a sense of the other is understanding who one's fellow citizens are. As such, it is the inverse of the sense of self, which pertains to the individual. Just as one must know what one believes about certain issues and understand one's preferences and character, one must also have some awareness of how others think about these matters. Firstly, one must be able to see how problems look to people with different backgrounds. As one student reflected, this ability is part of being a good citizen, because a good citizen is:

> someone who's involved and someone who is able to see the issue or problem from someone else's perspective. I sometimes hopelessly wish that everyone else [would] be able to see something from the other person's perspective. It seems simple but it's really, really difficult to do at times, either because you're just stuck in your own way of seeing things or just unable to understand where someone else is coming from.

Differences in people's circumstances can result in them having different perspectives in all kinds of ways. What may seem a perfectly sensible solution to a problem in one's own context might be quite unhelpful in another. Understanding the context in which others live can help one understand why that solution is inappropriate. One student gave an illuminating example of this:

> As a white person from the UK, I can look at the use of plastic in Indonesia or something and say, "They need to stop using plastic." But, hey, we need to stop using plastic [just] as much here. They're not in a financial situation at the moment where they can develop this technology. . . . Once industrialisation has fully occurred, then they'll be able to think more about being eco-conscious. You can't just look at people and say they need to be doing things this way. You have to look at the social environment in which they belong in order to understand their perspectives.

Secondly, having a developed sense of the other involves understanding their cultural norms, values, and ways of working. Inevitably, people from different backgrounds will have different expectations of how interpersonal interactions are supposed to go and will respond differently in different circumstances. Being aware of this, and being able to use this knowledge to regulate one's own behaviour, is important in today's world:

> Because especially in this ever-globalising world, you're bound to meet . . . at least with an academic degree, you're bound to run into people from other backgrounds. If you actually understand where they came from, it's so much easier to be successful. Like I said, with the Japanese way of going about a meeting, if you don't know them, and you go to a meeting in Japan, . . . it's way easier if you know their way of thinking and know how they do these things. Actually, I think it's not necessarily that it's absolutely necessary, but it will get you a lot further.

## The Sense of the Other as a Democratic Virtue

In a plural society, with citizens having different cultural backgrounds, opinions, and perspectives, being able to understand others makes it easier to take their interests into account in the governing process. This makes having a sense of the other a central democratic virtue. Recall that the fundamental idea of a democratic conversation is that citizens consider different perspectives and seek to determine the best solution for the community as a whole. An individual gives their independent assessment of what is in everyone's interest, considering their self-interest but also that of others. This is fostered by understanding other people's circumstances. Without this, it is difficult to grasp how others would be affected by certain measures. As one student explained:

> Maybe voting for this particular bill will affect people with low-income wages much more than it would [affect] you. Or even just things like electricity. . . . We want sustainable and all that, but then, now I'm much more inclined to think, "Oh, but people who are struggling a little bit more with their wages would be less likely to choose that because they can't afford it. It's not because they don't care about the environment, but because they just simply don't have the money." Rather than just condemning them and saying, "You're not sustainable." I can see that that's where they're coming from. I think that's what's relevant.

Not only must citizens have insight into the perspectives of others, but they must also be inclined to take those perspectives into account. After all, it is one thing to understand the viewpoints of others but quite another to care about their interests and give them weight in one's thinking. One might be a highly empathetic egoist, i.e., someone who has a good idea of where others are coming from, but who nevertheless ruthlessly pursues their self-interest and who might even use their knowledge of other people's circumstances to effectively pursue their own advantage. This would not be proper democratic behaviour. As discussed in Chapter 2, for democratic conversations to generate outcomes that can be regarded as legitimate by all members of society, citizens must not only argue for their self-interest, but they must also take a broad view and consider the interests of others and the community as a whole:

> I feel like if you're a good citizen, you must step away from your personal conviction sometimes and see it in a more, [a] broader picture. That's what liberal arts really teaches you. If you don't do that, then people will . . . , maybe they will only follow their own personal motivations and not see it in a broader sense. Whereas I think that broader sense is really necessary in order to make society go in the right direction.

Citizens must not only take the perspectives of others into account in an abstract sense, but they must also be able to participate in dialogue and exchange with fellow citizens about issues of common concern. They must be able to present arguments to each other and evaluate the arguments that others make. This is the essence of a democratic conversation. To do this, it can be very helpful to comprehend how others understand issues and what their arguments are so that one may address their assumptions and values:

> You also need to know, okay, why would they disagree with me in the first place? Is there a reason why they don't like my idea? Then you have to, yes, place yourself in the other person and then you also see okay, well, if I want to [ban the Qur'an], for instance, and I want to convince someone, what does that mean for the other person? To convince someone else of your argument you need to know why the other would be opposed to it in the first place.

## Teaching the Sense of the Other in the International Classroom

LAS programmes help students develop a sense of the other by offering them a highly international classroom. The students interviewed are firmly convinced of this. As one interviewee exclaimed when asked how liberal education helps students develop a sense of the other:

> How does liberal arts teach you [that]? That's the model!

LAS programmes typically have highly international student populations, with up to 60% of students coming from foreign countries, and more than 50 nationalities represented in many cases. Moreover, they typically seek to recruit students from all over the world, or at least all over Europe, and in recent years have tried to enrol students from a wider range of socio-economic backgrounds. However, this is not enough to help students develop a sense of the other. Rather, a combination of factors is needed to ensure students develop an understanding of each other's perspectives and backgrounds. Some of these have already been discussed. Nevertheless, they have a specific function in the context of the international classroom and as such warrant further consideration. Students pointed to three aspects of their education: the multidisciplinary curriculum, in which students look at issues from multiple disciplinary perspectives; the active pedagogy, in which students from many different countries and backgrounds actively exchange perspectives on the issues they are studying; and the emphasis on academic community, in which conversations that start in the classroom are often continued in a social, co-curricular context.

Students often remarked on how studying multiple disciplines helped them understand how people from different backgrounds might see the world differently. After all, each discipline identifies certain information as relevant, which leads to a particular perspective on issues. Studying different disciplines teaches one that the information one has shapes how one looks at matters:

> In terms of being on this course, I think the more I've gone through different disciplines, it has made me see how other people with different information understand the world in a different way.

Not only does studying a multidisciplinary curriculum help one see that others might have a different perspective, it can also help one understand how others might be affected by decisions in different ways. Students realise that solutions that are good from certain perspectives are bad from others, and this teaches them that what benefits some people, or even a majority of people, can be harmful to others:

> If you have multiple perspectives coming in, I think you're more likely to know what's in it for others, and therefore might be more likely to know what it might cost others, even if it's good for a majority. That's why you'd be more inclined to recognise how a collective decision, which is good for the vast majority of a country, for instance, might still have negative repercussions for a smaller group.

However, the most obvious way in which an international classroom helps students develop a sense of the other is by encouraging a diverse group of students to interact in the context of their education. Because students from many different backgrounds study together, they learn about other students' perspectives and, in the process, backgrounds. Typically, students talk about this in terms of the many nationalities that are represented in their programmes:

> I'm communicating more with international people than I have ever done. . . . So, for that project that we did on depression, we had a girl from France, a girl from Russia, [and] a boy from Romania. Then in another project, we had two French people, a Polish person, [and] a Colombian person, who I was translating for with my Spanish ability.

An international classroom is characterised by a certain style of interaction. Students must be encouraged to understand each other's contributions, rather than to falsify them. If one enters a classroom with the assumption that one's own way of seeing things is correct, and all other ways of looking at issues are therefore wrong, one will seek to prove that one is right. One will provide as many arguments for one's position as one can and try to find mistakes in the arguments others make. This makes it hard to truly understand how others think about issues. So, rather than resembling a competition, the international classroom should be a joint exploration of issues, in which every perspective is first understood before it is assessed. Of course, independence of thought requires that arguments be assessed critically, but they should be assessed in a generous fashion, with the aim of finding mutual understanding. LAS students, who are expected to always look at issues from different disciplinary perspectives, and who must find ways of making those different perspectives relate to each other, are very much inclined to take such an approach:

> I think doing liberal arts forces you to think outside of your own per-spective, and outside of your own approach to things. . . . You have to listen to what's needed, to what's required, to what you want to do with your different areas of study. Because you have to listen in order to understand and to adapt to different subjects. I think that very much applies as well to debate and chat. I think maybe liberal arts students will be more used to taking a pause, listening, and really having more of an interaction, because it's very much more about interacting with subjects within your studies, and it's also about interactive links. So, I think that does translate to the public sphere, and to you talking to people in a way that maybe you wouldn't if you just stuck to your little box.

An important aspect of interaction in an international classroom is that it allows students to correct each other's perceptions. Students often enter the classroom with assumptions about other cultures. These might be inaccu-rate and even insulting to people from those cultures. If one meaningfully interacts with people from such cultures, they can share their experiences and in that way remedy inaccurate preconceptions. While it may be frustrat-ing for them to have to deal with cultural stereotypes, this process is also experienced as highly meaningful. One student explained how their educa-tion helped them become friends with people from different social, cultural, and economic backgrounds:

> Yes, I really did that a lot. You don't have to, but I would like you to understand that sometimes for me, it really sucks, like, if I'm listening to somebody who is very privileged about any situation in their life. I have a multitude of very hurtful associations from my past when . . . [peo-ple say], "Oh God, I really wanted also to learn about Asian culture.", "When I was 10, I wanted to live in Africa." etcetera. If I acknowledge that feeling and set it aside, and sit in the conversation, and act in it, I really get to learn from this person, and we get into dialogue. Then

I say, "I know something about underprivileged communities via experiencing [them]. What did you think about this?" Just the process of negotiating a situation with them, I find it very interesting.

However, the international classroom is not limited to the classroom. The interaction between different students, in which they seek to explore each other's perspectives and backgrounds, may start in a formal setting. But since LAS programmes seek to be true academic communities, in which curricular and extra-curricular activities are linked, and in which students continuously interact in a social context, conversations that start in the classroom can be continued outside of formal education. This allows students to get to know each other in a meaningful way and to become friends; they can observe the differences between themselves, including differences of opinions, in ways of working, and of culture, and learn how to get along well:

> Oftentimes when you're in class, you do discuss the readings, but you also go outside the readings to discuss. People talk about their personal lives and then you have your friends, . . . your colleagues, [who are] perhaps more important than the class curriculum itself. Able to see people like that and then still be able to be their friends is [such a] transcendent point, . . . I find. I'm so different from a lot of the people, we come from such different backgrounds. Everything is different. Even the way we use the language. Even our vocabulary, everything. Then, at the same time, we're still able to become friends. I think that that's some greater understanding, some compromise that we have all collectively [made], so that we can still, we're not fighting each other on campus or whatever.

Of course, students do experience tensions in seeking to understand each other's perspectives. While they report that they often acquire a greater understanding of, and sympathy for, the views of others, they also believe that certain perspectives are simply not acceptable. The strong convictions many have on issues make it hard for them to give credence to certain views or arguments, for example, those that appear racist or that promote inequality. This results in friction between their sense of self and their developing sense of the other, something that several students were acutely aware of:

> I think I want to meet more people who are really different from me, but I . . . strongly believe that it's important to not be racist, for example, so I don't know. I don't know how exactly to empathise with people

who are different from me in that respect when it's something that also matters to me quite a lot.

This was perhaps more of a theoretical concern for many students. LAS programmes are, by and large, liberal, progressive communities. Even though students in these programmes come from many countries, and represent a huge diversity of experience and perspectives, LAS student populations are homogenous in other respects. Here, too, students were acutely aware that this is problematic if programmes really wish to help students develop a sense of the other. Indeed, many students expressed a desire for more diversity in the community and for the presence of students who represent perspectives that many would not agree with:

> One thing people often say is conservative people, or right-wing people, shouldn't come, but I think it's the most fun if they come here, because otherwise, you're just in this very, very left-wing bubble. . . . What liberal arts and sciences is about is [that] you see things from different perspectives, but sometimes I feel like because it's so left-wing here, that, I'm left-wing myself, but still, people go a bit too far in it and don't see the reasoning of right-wing perspectives anymore. I always think it's fun if someone who has a different view on things comes along.

Students recognise that while LAS programmes certainly help students develop a sense of the other, a truly international classroom requires a genuinely diverse student population in more respects than just nationality. However pleasant it might be to study among people with similar perspectives, as future citizens, students will have to govern together with people who have very different views. For this, it will be helpful if they understand those people, or at least have the ability to learn about the different perspectives they have. Hence, LAS programmes should make more of an effort to achieve a truly diverse student population. However, even in its imperfect form, an international classroom, with all that it entails, can help students develop this sense of the other:

> because I think there's a big part, at least of our programme, which is talking to other students about what they do, talking to other students about their courses, talking about what their philosophy on life is. You actually discover a lot about the world and about all these diverse perspectives, since we all come from different parts of Europe. You get to know people very well, and I think that develops you as a person. It definitely changed me.

# Note

1 The term international classroom is something of a misnomer, in part because it refers to more than just interaction in the classroom, but also because it suggests that diversity in nationality is all that matters. While this is an important dimension of the diversity that the ideal requires, other kinds of diversity, for example in terms of culture, socio-economic background, or ideology, are just as valuable. However, since the term is often used, it will be adopted here.

# 8   Compromise and Group Work

*Participating with people from different disciplines in projects, for example, with people with vastly different viewpoints, gives you the ability to, for example, not only understand people's viewpoints that come from different disciplines, but also to make compromises and communicate non-violently. . . . It's a bit of a weird term but I think it makes sense, where you, we have an actual discussion and not a debate where you try to just win and convince somebody of your argument, but where you [do] as you do in a dialogue. For example, you take the other standpoint. You maybe disagree with certain arguments. You [re-phrase] it in a more charitable way and maybe find some common ground, and then you can agree on something. That's something – that's a skill that you can't learn in a one-semester course. You have to do it and then do it again, and get feedback and get re-evaluated, make your own experiences. That's something that this liberal arts programme's done for me for a long time.*

When living together with other people and when making collective decisions with others, one cannot always get one's way. Given the plural nature of modern society and the differences between people, both in terms of their interests and their conceptions of the common good, there is unlikely to be spontaneous agreement. Democratic conversations are all about negotiating these differences and overcoming them. This requires compromise. Citizens must come to agreements about what is to be done, and they must regard these agreements as, in some sense, legitimate, so that they feel committed to them.

Genuine compromise is difficult, as is apparent from the political polarisation that characterises much of contemporary politics. Different parties and factions rarely manage to reach agreements, preferring to emphasise their differences and to attack each other's arguments. And even in more mundane contexts, disagreements are often hard to resolve. This is understandable. If one has a certain view and has thought hard about the issue, one's first instinct is often to defend that view and to seek to convince those

DOI: 10.4324/9781003336594-8

who have a different opinion. However, if everyone does this, one no longer has a genuinely democratic conversation, but rather a competition. This is unlikely to result in a mutually agreeable solution and might very well end in frustration:

> I had a conversation with my sister who has a job and she said, "You know the person that I'm working with is not from around here and whenever we speak, I accidentally insult him, and he accidentally insults me. Then we both get mad, and we leave the room."

Reaching a genuine compromise requires one to change one's mind, and it requires finding solutions that no one had initially thought of but that everyone ends up regarding as their own.

Compromise is a skill which one must develop, and LAS students feel that their education helps them cultivate this ability. One experience they believe helps them learn the art of compromise is group work. Many LAS programmes require students to work together on scholarly projects, including research, papers, and presentations. While students sometimes find group work frustrating, they recognise that not only discussing matters with others but actually working together over a sustained period helps them overcome their differences and find a genuine synthesis of their initial views. The student quoted above continued:

> I think what liberal arts . . . has taught me is to not really leave the room. To stay in it and to really just continue discussing, and continue learning, and to make something happen. If you keep it at the level of just discussion and you never either write it down or create a project, you don't realise the implications of whatever it is that you were discussing.[1]

## Compromise

The essence of compromise is negotiating differences of opinion to come to a joint conclusion. Reaching a joint conclusion is not agreeing to disagree; agreeing to disagree does not result in a particular course of action or a solution, which is what democratic governance is supposed to provide. Nor is reaching a joint conclusion the result of mechanically splitting the difference, i.e., giving everyone a bit of what they want and being done with it. Of course, genuine compromise does involve give and take, and while no one will get everything they would like, everyone should get something. Importantly, however, the outcome should be a true synthesis of different people's perspectives, an outcome that each one of them has contributed to. Each party must seek to see the validity of others' views; they may perhaps have to change their minds on certain matters, and they must ultimately propose solutions that, as far as possible, do justice to all concerned. For that reason, everyone can regard the solution as co-created and, in that way, legitimate.

Compromise is closely related to the other civic virtues discussed so far. After looking at social issues in an open-minded way, considering different disciplinary perspectives, and interrogating those perspectives with independence of thought, one can come to one's own conclusions, which contributes to a sense of self. One will have invested a lot of energy and effort into developing one's views, and so one is likely also to have a considerable commitment to them. Hence, one might initially find it perplexing that other people do not see things the same way:

> When you're studying here, in the beginning, you really start to form your values. You [become] more informed and start to share [your] political stance and then you realise that it clashes with certain types of people. That it clashes with the perspectives of others. I always wonder sometimes, why do they not just think like us? Why don't they just go for this way of life, because we deem it the best or we deem it the most interesting, the most fun.

A sense of the other can help one appreciate why others have different perspectives. However, understanding another perspective is different from agreeing with it. Compromise also involves being willing to reconsider one's view and to incorporate new information that one might not have taken into account. This is not easy. It involves revising one's own opinion and weighing different arguments and perspectives. However, if done in good faith, it can result in better solutions:

> Being able to talk about issues and differences is one thing and being able to convince someone, and convince someone fairly, justly, is something else completely. You both have your facts, you both have your evidence, and you both have your conclusion, which is probably very great and grounded within your own field of study. . . . I think that's the eternal discussion that you then should have: "Okay, so why is my answer different, and is [there] maybe anything I missed, or are we able to come to a joint conclusion which is even better?"

## Compromise as a Democratic Virtue

Being able to reach compromises is a quintessential democratic virtue. The entire democratic process is about talking through different opinions and interests to come to a collective decision. In a democratic conversation, individuals present their different perspectives on common problems, listen to the perspectives of others, and then, crucially, decide on a concrete course of action. Given the fact that different individuals look at matters differently, some convergence is required to reach an actionable conclusion. Indeed, this convergence is what enables democratic conversations to result in legitimate outcomes; it is because individuals participate in the process of compromise that they are able to feel like joint authors of the eventual decision. If, after having heard each participant's perspective, a simple vote was to be taken to select a single viewpoint to implement, those who do not share that view would have little reason to regard the decision as legitimate. It is by seeking a compromise that a governing process can produce outcomes that do the most justice to all perspectives concerned.

In a democratic conversation, the ability to compromise is crucial. Those who are unable or unwilling to compromise will turn any such conversation into a competition, in which their overarching goal is to vindicate their own positions. They will make the process into an adversarial negotiation, in which they are more concerned with the submission of other participants than with finding a fair solution for all concerned. This makes the democratic arena into a boxing ring. Being able to find a compromise ensures democratic conversations do not become contests and allows participants to resolve disputes in all kinds of settings. As one student put it when explaining what can go wrong if a disagreement turns into a competition:

> It's easy to shut off and become rude, but I feel like here we learn to create a peaceful and rich atmosphere of communication. I feel like I can take that to a lot of different settings. [For example,] at home, there is some dispute between my mom and brother about whether they communicate [or do] house chores, and I feel like [there], the same skills of listening and understanding different sides help a lot.

The "peaceful and rich" atmosphere of LAS programmes is sustained by a culture in which compromising is valued and students must sometimes admit that their initial views were problematic. People must believe:

> that not being 100% dogmatic yourself doesn't mean that you are weak, and at the same time, the person in front of you who is talking, [just] because they sound good, [doesn't] mean that you can't argue back towards them. It does teach you to argue with that confidence [that] it's okay that there are so many other points of view, and that it's okay if you turn out to be wrong as well.

This attitude is essential for a proper democratic conversation. Those who are entirely dogmatic and unwilling to admit that they are occasionally wrong will not be able to regard democratic solutions as legitimate. They may concede that they were outvoted or lost the debate, but they will not consider the conclusions as their own:

> You have to accept that at some point your opinion and what you think is the most important thing should not always be the most important thing for others. You have to learn to subordinate at some point. That's really important.

However, this subordination is not a negative thing, an unavoidable cost of living together with others in society. Those who are willing to compromise will find that doing so brings them together and reminds them of common ground. Compromises unite different people, making them feel that the conclusion of a democratic conversation belongs to everyone and for that reason can be regarded as legitimate by everyone. One student put this well, remarking that studying LAS helps people see that:

> compromise is a nice thing because you get to solutions that connect people and . . . they connect, and they may give people common ground. [In terms of] character, compromise is super fun, also to realise, okay, we share that, and it shows you where [what] you think and what you are is different, also because a compromise means at first being confronted with difference. But now it means that you are also [connected]. Because compromises also always incorporate some bits of both opinions.

## Teaching Compromise Through Group Work

Students in LAS programmes believe their education makes them more able to find compromises. Many of the features of liberal education already discussed contribute to this ability. For example, a multidisciplinary curriculum can help one find and accept compromises by promoting open-mindedness and a sense of the other. Seeing the value of other perspectives and understanding why others might look at the world differently can make one see that a good solution does justice to the complexity of different viewpoints. Those who have studied only a single discipline are much more likely only to be able to see the world from that disciplinary perspective and to believe it to provide the only valid understanding of a given problem. For such people, compromise can be difficult, in contrast to those who have learned to see things from multiple points of view:

> Because you have a multidisciplinary background, you are more likely to understand other people's perspectives. Not necessarily agree, but especially understand it, where it's coming from, what it's based on. In that sense, I think you might be more inclined to go for a compromise, and also accept that compromise, because you understand their positions, rather than just being like, "No, this is what I have learned. This is right because I read it in a textbook. I'm not going to compromise, because this is how I think of it."

Moreover, an active pedagogy, especially in the context of the international classroom, is very conducive to learning how to compromise. In a lecture-based system of education, students are not confronted with the differences in perspective that exist between them, nor are they invited to resolve those differences. When students come from a wide range of backgrounds, there are likely to be profound disagreements. While it could be argued that a classroom discussion might simply make those disagreements visible, in fact, such discussions often lead to compromises. In an active LAS classroom, it is considered unsatisfying merely to note how individuals with different backgrounds look at matters:

> It is very interesting to go into a tutorial where you discuss something, and yes, you have readings, but on top of that, you will have had different experiences. You'll have had different family, and national, and geographical, and cultural backgrounds, and they do clash. Sometimes you'll have to compromise. . . . I remember taking [the course contemporary] history and we had a student from Belarus, and we had an American exchange student taking the class. It was a [session] on neoliberal values, and that was really interesting to see and also to see how over the course of the two hours . . .
> Q: Did they do more than agree to disagree?
> Yes, they did. They did agree that they both had points too. In the end, you become more, it's still through communication that you deal with these things and that people are more inclined, I don't know why it is exactly that people are inclined to it, but very often there will be cooperation afterwards or they will have beers over it and then will be like, "Yes, super interesting."

However, the main way in which LAS programmes help students develop the ability to compromise is through group work. These programmes typically require groups of students to complete assignments together. This might include conducting research projects, writing substantial reports and papers, or preparing presentations. Oftentimes, these group assignments take weeks or even months, and they require substantial initiative from the students, both in terms of organisation and in terms of content. Crucially, the students involved must produce a unified piece of work that they all stand behind and are all assessed on. It is easy to see how this requires students to compromise. Students who only do assignments and exams individually are never required to negotiate different answers and perspectives but are merely required to present their own answers. However, when doing group work, different students will likely want to take the project in different directions or will have different ideas concerning the conclusion. This necessitates some sort of compromise:

> Sure, sometimes you're in a group and you all have the same vision, and you want to work on this one thing in pretty much the same way, perfect, . . . and sometimes you're a bunch of people who all have their own ideas. Everyone wants to do their thing and then you need to find a way to work with that, to reconcile those different ideas.

Oftentimes, students find group projects deeply frustrating. While they recognise the value of learning how to work together effectively, they frequently comment on how working together with others can be difficult. In part, this relates to the process of working together, with tensions often caused by individuals' different working styles. After all, students differ in how they like to work, approach deadlines, handle stress, and the like. Finding ways of working that everyone finds acceptable is a key democratic challenge. In the process, students learn to compromise:

> Some students really like being in the background, but really do the work when you need them to do the work. Others are really dominant in the beginning, and really want all of these things done but then pull back as soon as the stress hits. I think that [in] navigating that, everyone has a different view of how things should be done, and then trying to make that work and compromising, and finding a solution to that, is much more helpful than me writing an essay on my own or a paper and then presenting it.

The challenges and frustrations of group work are not limited to the process of working together. They also pertain to the content of projects. Different students will have different opinions about the issues under consideration.

They will have invested considerable effort into developing those opinions and may be reluctant to abandon them:

> I sometimes think group work is even harder here than it was in high school . . . because people are so opinionated and so used to forming their own opinions very specifically.

These different opinions need to be reconciled or the group project cannot be completed. Differences need to be considered and weighed in a collaborative process, with the implications of potential solutions examined from each participant's perspective. In doing so, aspects of different perspectives must be discarded, while consensus forms around particular ideas. Students described this as a process of negotiation, where negotiation means:

> to think within yourself of all the implications something has for you and to think with others of all the implications that it has for them . . . and then you're like, "Okay, these are things that we really like. [These are] the things that we were unclear about, the things that we don't like, this is the context." That's negotiation for me, so understanding.

This process of negotiation, in the end, must lead to a synthesis of different views and a conclusion that everyone can stand behind. The synthesis is often not what a given individual had initially intended. However, each individual realises that the synthesis is also not what others had intended. Everyone will have explored the perspectives of the others and reconsidered their own viewpoints in that light. This can lead to a co-created compromise, one that everyone can regard as their own. One student, who had to complete their final thesis in a group, explained this process evocatively:

> We also have to do a thesis, and I already did it, and you have to do it with other students, and you have to arrive at a common conclusion. You are writing separate chapters with different disciplinary backgrounds, but you are [supposed] to integrate them. Most academics, or many academics, at least in history and economics and so on, are used to writing a paper on their own and with their own perspectives, and you are saying, "These are the perspectives of others, and this is what I have to say. This is my opinion." You also have to do that in this thesis, but you also had to make that compatible with what other people are saying and arrive at a common conclusion. That is not always something that completely reflects your own thoughts. In that sense, I had to compromise some. I'm sure, I know my fellow students also had to compromise somewhat in terms of the answer. I think I learned

from that to, or I developed my ability to empathise with what other people have to say and take that into account, or to think again, and think about my own assumptions and opinions again, with help of that input. I would say that is something you could learn from, for example, writing such a thesis.

Group work is thus instrumental in helping students develop the ability to compromise. They are forced not only to think about their own perspectives but must also consider the perspectives of others and reconcile all these views. They must do so in a constructive fashion. They cannot resort to platitudes but must produce a coherent conclusion that they can all accept. Going through this process makes students less dogmatic and more able to find compromises. If they can reach compromises during their education, they will be able to do so when engaging in democratic conversations as citizens. For there, too, they will have to consider the views of others, negotiate differences, and find a synthesis that they can regard as legitimate. If they cannot do so, they will frustrate and undermine democratic conversations, turning democracy into a battle of wills that promises to leave everyone dissatisfied. This realisation is perhaps the greatest lesson group work can teach:

> Just working with other people at some point you realise, "Okay, it's not going to work the way you wanted it to." Or if you have to write a paper with someone and you have a whole plan, and then they're just like, "No, I don't really feel like doing that." At some point, you just have to accept that, "Okay, I can't just trailblaze my way through my degree or my life, I have to see other people's opinions and feelings, and take those into account."

## Note

1  Also appears in Teun Dekker, "Generic Skills Development in European Liberal Arts and Sciences Programmes: A Student Perspective," (Forthcoming).

## Reference

Dekker, Teun. "Generic Skills Development in European Liberal Arts and Sciences Programmes: A Student Perspective." (Forthcoming).

# 9 Knowledge of Social Issues and General Education

*Well, in my view, a good citizen in a democratic society is a citizen that's a little bit aware of what's happening around [them]. With liberal arts, it's also a lot of what current issues . . . are happening, so in that sense, it makes you a good democratic citizen.*

Winston Churchill once said that the best argument against democracy is five minutes with the average voter. In making this quip, he was echoing one of the oldest critiques of democracy, already made by Plato, that most citizens are not particularly well-informed about the problems that face society, what can be done about them, or even how the political process works.[1] Hence, they can hardly be expected to contribute to resolving these problems. Advocates of democracy can offer a range of responses to this critique. They might argue that the large numbers of citizens involved in a democracy make up for many being ill-informed, that in selecting goals for society no specialist knowledge is required, or that it is better to be ruled by less knowledgeable citizens than by corrupt elites. Nevertheless, it seems obvious that to fulfil their role well, citizens should at least be somewhat informed about social problems and current affairs. If they are aware of relevant information and have a basic understanding of the issues, they will be able to make more meaningful contributions to democratic conversations and will find it easier to understand and assess the contributions of others. However, if citizens have little or inaccurate knowledge of the issues under discussion, it will be harder for democratic conversations to yield good outcomes. As one student explained:

When your mental framework is based on inaccurate information, then the consequences can be fairly big. You need to be aware of what's around you and what the consequences of you voting or of you doing certain things, deciding on certain things, could be. You have to be informed [about] current events.

DOI: 10.4324/9781003336594-9

In contemporary society, participants in the democratic process are not always adequately informed about the challenges society faces. Perhaps due to a lack of education, disinterest, or the proliferation of inaccurate information on social media, many democratic conversations are plagued by a lack of knowledge of social issues.

Education, and certainly higher education, is well-placed to do something about this. But while some university programmes focus on social challenges, many traditional, mono-disciplinary programmes do not, regarding this as outside their remit. From a democratic perspective, this is a missed opportunity. LAS education, in contrast, offers an educational model that allows students to develop an interest in social issues and to acquire knowledge of current affairs. In large part, this is due to the content of the courses, which frequently address social challenges and contemporary issues. Studying these issues awakens students' desire to learn about them:

> Now the news is a part of my routine every day. Three years ago, before I started this degree, it really wasn't. . . .
>
> Q: Was it the curriculum that did that? Were there other people? Was it the community, or was it . . . ?
>
> I think the curriculum. I think that the more [news stories], and topics, and things that are addressed, the more aware you become of the scope of things you have yet to explore, and the more curious you become.

While many courses offered at LAS programmes deal with social issues, many do not. However, these programmes typically require students to complete a general education requirement: every student in LAS programmes must complete several courses outside of their areas of concentration or major, usually including core courses and a distribution requirement. While different programmes have different policies, and general education can serve a number of educational purposes, many students find that these courses inform them about contemporary issues and stimulate them to take an interest in current affairs. As one student explained when asked how LAS could teach social or personal skills, or even make one a good person:

> I think by having the core courses, that's a good step. To make sure that we all have knowledge of some basic disciplines: philosophy of science, political philosophy, history, and then science, how science works. . . .
>
> Q: That doesn't make you a [good person, does it?]
>
> It gives you exposure, exposure to new questions, important questions, and then you can reflect on them when you go home.

## Knowledge of Social Issues

Knowledge of social issues can refer to a whole host of things. The general idea is that one should have some understanding of the problems and challenges facing society, and of one's role in dealing with them:

> I think on the one hand, of course, we learned about collective action and how every individual contributing is important, but then you also end up learning about these huge problems that are difficult to solve.

Important issues that demand social action include climate change, social inequality, public health, international security, migration, and globalisation. Citizens need to be aware of relevant facts and ways of understanding these issues and use this information in their contributions to democratic conversations:

> What's a good citizen? I don't know. It's just someone that remains informed, through diverse types of channels of information, has a critical eye for statistics and studies, and someone who participates in local politics, like politics on a personal level, immediately around you, as well as the more direct democracy stuff.

On the one hand, an understanding of current affairs is something one can develop by following the news in the media. On the other hand, such an understanding can involve more academic, theoretical knowledge that one might gain at university. Both are important and can even reinforce each other: having academic knowledge can make it easy to understand or be interested in what one reads in the press and being aware of the news can help one understand more abstract theories or concepts. In addition to this, citizens should know about the political process and the initiatives that are underway to deal with social issues. As one student explained when asked what knowledge a good citizen should have:

> Well, know your political leaders, know a little bit what they stand for. Know the conservatives, liberals. Know which party does what, know a little bit about what happens in the world. Just big events and, mainly, events that influence you as a person.

Of course, one might distinguish between knowledge of global social issues, which affect multiple political communities, and local social issues relating to one's immediate surroundings. While it is important to understand global issues, it is no less important to be aware of local ones, if only because these are the issues on which citizens can have the biggest impact:

> I think . . . that being conscious [of] your own locality is sometimes more important than focusing on global issues because none of us can really change that individually, but you can make a difference to your neighbourhood, and your country, and whatever.

Knowledge of social issues serves as input for democratic conversations, building on the five democratic virtues discussed so far. Having knowledge of social issues is what allows one to look at different perspectives on issues in an open-minded but independent way, to develop one's own position on them, to understand the perspectives of others, and, ultimately, to compromise. As such, being a good citizen requires:

> having a reasonable selection of information and also information sources, and then perhaps some multitude of narratives to understand also what the debates are about, and not just having a preformed opinion, but also knowing about a topic and forming your opinion yourself. Perhaps that is what good citizenship is about.

## Knowledge of Social Issues as a Democratic Virtue

It is perhaps too obvious to be worth stating that having some knowledge of social issues helps one fulfil one's role as a citizen. The entire concept of democracy is based on the idea that citizens are in a good position to provide meaningful input into the governing process, and this requires them to be well-informed. If no one has even a rudimentary understanding of the problems society faces, then it is unlikely that a good collective solution to those problems can be found.

Of course, the problems contemporary society faces are too complex for even the most well-informed citizens to completely understand. But, while complete mastery is not required, some understanding of the issues is a good thing because it helps citizens provide direction to the government. Recall the view that a democratic conversation can lead to good outcomes because it pools the wisdom of many citizens. The arguments for this contention, including the jury theorem, acknowledge that increasing the competence of the participants, by providing them with more and better knowledge, is beneficial. If nobody in a democratic conversation has any knowledge of the issues, there is nothing to pool:

> I think to make this sort of idea that we have of democracy, as a representation of the people, work, you have to know what's going on.

Moreover, democratic conversations eventually must lead to some conclusion, which requires a decision-making procedure, usually some sort of vote. Those who do not have the slightest idea of current events will find it hard to decide what to vote in any sensible fashion, or they might vote in ways that they would regret if they were better informed. As voting is the most obvious way in which citizens participate in the governance of their societies on a national level in contemporary democracy, this is highly relevant. The democratic ideal requires that they think carefully about which party or candidate might serve society best, as they understand it. For this, understanding social issues is crucial. If individuals are not voting on an informed basis, the democratic system is not functioning as intended, and one may wonder if democracy is a good form of government:

> I find voting very important, but informed voting. I find it very difficult to personally, sort of, I would say be at peace with the fact that . . . a lot of people go into the voting booth very uninformed about the consequences their vote may have, and the basis on which they're voting might not be as broad as I [would] wish it to be, which is maybe a sort of, a little bit too [much of a] snobby comment, but I think that doesn't serve our public interest in the best way.

Citizens also shape their societies in more local and mundane contexts. Interactions with fellow members of society, however minor, offer an opportunity for debating issues and can shape opinions. These, too, are effectively democratic conversations, and they inform actual political activity. However, even these kinds of interactions are only possible if citizens are at least somewhat informed about the issues affecting society. They would have nothing to discuss otherwise:

> It's important to stay informed about current events . . . for multiple reasons. One reason is . . . it really helps you in daily life. If you want to have contact with anybody whatsoever, from the bakery to your work, if you have a current event, it always works.

Not taking opportunities to learn about current affairs poses great risks for democracy. Problematic developments can go unnoticed, and issues that affect certain members of society may not be addressed. Social problems might well get worse, to the detriment of the community, leading individuals to embrace radical political movements. The health of a democracy depends on citizens knowing what is going on because:

> I think if you ignore current events, and you don't face them, and you don't talk about them, you don't discuss them, then they can very easily

either be swept under the rug or they just accumulate, accumulate, accumulate.

## Teaching Knowledge of Social Issues Through General Education

Liberal education provides a model for how education can help students acquire knowledge of social issues. In part, this is because LAS programmes tend to have a culture in which an interest in current affairs is expected. They seek to be true academic communities, in which students interact outside of the classroom in the context of extra-curricular events. Moreover, these programmes tend to be relatively small, certainly compared to many traditional programmes, and often have dedicated buildings or facilities where students can socialise, such as common rooms or shared study lounges. This ensures a high level of social density; students tend to know each other well and are not anonymous passers-by. As a result, students are always running into each other and have frequent conversations about all kinds of topics. Many of these conversations end up being about current affairs:

> You . . . keep having conversations about topics, not necessarily things you discuss in class, but just things that pop up in the news, interesting stuff you read. "By the way did you hear about 'blah blah'?" The entire conversation erupts, about this and that factoring in, and, "What about?", "Remember that and that?", "I see some patterns from history. By the way, did you know that this and this happened before?" Everything is just related to the topic; it just keeps on floating around and I think that never ends. I think that especially intensifies what we are doing. It's not active studying, it's just that you keep having interactions with fields and things, and just mundane things that happen and then put them into context, basically immediately. Because someone brings it up and you're just like, "Oh yes."

However, the main way in which LAS programmes help students acquire knowledge of social issues is by requiring all students to complete a range of general education courses, which often expose students to theories and research about global challenges, recent history, and political matters. As a result, every graduate will have learnt about such issues, but may also have developed an interest in current affairs that they take with them as they fulfil their role as citizens.

Recall that liberal education expects students to study both a lot about a little and a little about a lot; the curriculum combines depth and breadth. The depth is provided by the concentration or major, while the breadth is catered for by a general education requirement. This general education curriculum typically consists of a number of core courses that all students must complete and a distribution requirement, which requires students to complete courses in domains and disciplines outside of their areas of concentration. Many traditional programmes in Europe that focus on specific disciplines or particular professions do not require students to take these kinds of courses. Students who study physics only study physics, whereas students studying physics in the context of a LAS programme will also be exposed to the general education curriculum.

Different LAS programmes have different general education programmes, with different core courses and different distribution requirements. Moreover, depending on the programme, the general education requirement serves many purposes. Programmes may aim to ensure students are familiar with scientific methodology, can approach scientific questions in an interdisciplinary fashion, or can work together with colleagues who have concentrated on different disciplines. However, students often report that these courses help them understand social issues better and foster an interest in current affairs.

Some programmes have core requirements that explicitly focus on thematic issues that are deemed to be of social concern. For example, programmes might require students to take courses pertaining to various global problems, such as environmental change, global health, or issues in international justice. Such courses quite obviously help students acquire academic knowledge about these issues. However, they also help students realise how important it is to think about these matters, making them more inclined to learn about social questions in the future:

> If I hadn't done all these global challenges [courses] in my first year, if I hadn't explored all these different really, really big issues of the world, I think the aspect of [thinking about] what the world really needs and how I can contribute to that would [be missing from] . . . my life. Yes, I think through liberal arts, I've realised that's something I want to do in life. Otherwise, it would feel, I wouldn't say useless, but I would say something would [be missing]. I would miss out on something. The world would miss out on something because I'm good at something that I'm not sharing with the world.

Other programmes require all students to take courses in modern history or political philosophy, based on the conviction that historical developments and central concepts of politics, such as justice or equality, inform both current events and scientific developments. Such courses give students the background they need to better understand contemporary social issues:

> In the core courses, I think I can see some tendency to make citizens democratically aware, I think. For example, let's look at political philosophy

and contemporary history. Those both make the students, who come from [the programme] and go into the world, more aware of these nuances of politics and ideologies, but also aware of the recent historical and political developments in the world in the last [few] years.

Even courses that are not explicitly about social issues can nevertheless stimulate students to think about current affairs if they provide them with concepts that help them understand the issues:

> The first class that I took here was about modern freedom and we think about what freedom [is], what has it been over the years, and what is it now, and what does it mean for me, but also for others. If you ask this question and you ask [it] the whole time through your studies, you cannot not think about democracy and about contemporary political issues.

An alternative way of conceptualising the core curriculum in LAS education is provided by the so-called great books tradition. In this tradition, studying certain canonical texts is the key feature of liberal arts. Students are made familiar with the books that have shaped society and have proven to possess an enduring legacy. While there is some disagreement about exactly which books are great, students are typically expected to study the ancient Greeks and Romans, certain religious texts, works of Renaissance literature, as well as books from the Enlightenment and Romantic periods. In an extreme version of such a curriculum, almost all of students' education consists of reading and discussing great books, as is the case at, for example, St. John's College in the US. However, there are quite a few LAS programmes in the world that require all students to take a few great books courses as part of the core curriculum.

Devotees of the great books approach sometimes argue that it is superior to the more topical or disciplinary approaches discussed above because it provides students with an understanding of the highlights of human achievement that they can use to orient themselves in dealing with the problems they will face in society. Rather than studying social problems directly, or disciplines that can help one understand them, students should immerse themselves in the best that humanity has produced, as this will inspire and equip them to make a valuable contribution to solving social issues. Eva Brann, a prominent advocate of this approach, once expressed this argument as follows:

> I think most of my colleagues have the sense that the world with all its troubles is best served by those of its inhabitants who are imbued with what is noble, high, and good, and who have occupied themselves with

theories and visions of what is best in the face of all that can go wrong – better than by those who have made a study of specific and current problems. The best preparation, we think, for doing good is not the somewhat spurious experience of social ills and personal badness that students are provided with in academic settings but the genuine absorption in excellence that liberal education naturally induces. In short, long liberal reflection on the way things ought to be is a better prelude to real life than a premature immersion in the worst facts of life.[2]

However, for better or for worse, the great books approach is not prominent in Europe; only one or two programmes make it a signature feature of their curricula, and none of the programmes at which students were interviewed had a core curriculum based on great books. Nevertheless, during the interviews, the great books approach occasionally came up. Often it was raised as an example to challenge students' conceptions of liberal education. In most cases, the idea did not resonate with students. Many were quite dismissive of it. For example, when a student was confronted with the example of St. John's College and was asked whether they would consider this a LAS programme, the answer was:

No. [It] depends how you do it, but that wouldn't be enough to be called liberal arts. It's interesting, you can do that in your free time, or you can set up a club and read such a book every month. I just don't see how you can base, or why you should base, your [education on that].

Perhaps students in European LAS programmes are sceptical of the great books approach, in which a pre-determined list of canonical texts structures the curriculum, because it does not sit well with the freedom of choice that characterises their education. The individualised approach that many programmes in Europe champion, which is based on the idea that every student has their own needs and interests, is seemingly incompatible with the notion that certain books are objectively great and universally valuable:

I think, for me, this idea that there is great research, or a canon, or something that is essential, whereas other things are not, I think [this] is not true, because I think we all have different things that we need to focus on to really find our place, where we are needed, or where we can make a difference, or have an impact, or just be happy, to be honest.

Some students argued that the great books approach is too Western in nature and that it focuses on books that are the product of histories that are oppressive. In the age of decolonisation of the curriculum, making these books the centrepiece of a LAS programme was thought to be problematic. The student quoted above continued:

> Also, there's a real tendency with this great books tradition, or great research, or whatever, that it becomes very Eurocentric, which I think is a huge issue . . . [in higher] education in general, and [in] university education. What we define as great is really defined by histories that I disagree with, and I think we need to break out of that.

Despite this, European LAS programmes do offer courses which take a great books approach, even though they do not make them compulsory. Students who took these courses reported seeing their value, including in the context of civic education. One student argued that these books, which have stood the test of time, can teach students about human nature precisely because their longevity shows that they reflect some universal truth about the human condition:

> They are part of liberal education because, I think, a liberal arts educa-tion is about becoming a good citizen, and becoming good at logic, and good at rhetoric, as I said. I think these books, the lessons that were learned from these books, have lasted until today, and that means they are of great value. Either you like or don't like the content. [But] they've lasted until today, and there is a reason that they lasted until today. Maybe people selected them randomly, but I don't think so. I think it's because there's actually something of substance inside that you can learn about human nature and beyond.

Hence, a great books approach within the core curriculum might very well help students develop knowledge of social issues and cultivate civic virtue. It would be worth experimenting with this more extensively. However, as things stand in Europe, this tradition has not taken root within the LAS movement, and as such cannot feature in an argument about the potential of this movement to teach civic virtue.

The distribution requirement that European LAS programmes typically ask students to complete, in addition to core courses, can also take many forms. The basic idea is that students should also study disciplines outside their main areas of focus so that they get at least some understanding of the main domains of science. A common way of doing this is by grouping the available courses into natural sciences, social sciences, and humanities, and asking students to complete courses in all three areas.

All students will therefore do at least some courses in the social sciences. Because the social sciences explicitly study social issues, all students will gain at least some knowledge that they can use to understand current affairs:

> It makes you more educated on a broader scale, so even if you are very science-ey or you said, "I'm very science orientated." you do have to take one of each subject at least in the first semester. You do have to take a politics course, or you do have to take something that is very applicable in modern-day life, and something that will maybe give you information that you [wouldn't] have before.

Of course, not everyone who takes one social science course will gain significant knowledge of social issues or develop an interest in current affairs that they carry with them for the rest of their lives. As one student pointed out somewhat jadedly:

> I think even though every student does have to do their mandatory one social science class, there are many people that choose to never ever do that again and choose to continue to not watch the news and continue to not want to be involved, because . . . they're happy with their lives and they don't really care if the world is shit for other people.

However, the same student acknowledged that in most cases, even students who do not focus on the social sciences are inspired by the experience, and do develop an interest in current affairs:

> You do have that percentage of people, but I do think that the majority of people at liberal arts and sciences colleges, they will have that one [course] and be like, "Wow, this is really what it's like and this is really what's happening." And they [will] want to take more of those classes even if it's not [their] major or something.

Having distribution requirements also means that all LAS students take at least some courses in the humanities. Humanities disciplines, including literature, cultural studies, and gender theory, study human thought and the products of human civilisation. They help students reflect on how narratives shape society, and how the way one thinks about issues influences how one relates to other people, but also how one treats them. Having some awareness of these matters can help citizens reflect critically on the issues contemporary society is facing, and in particular how those issues affect others:

> One of the key elements of the humanities is narratives, and talking, and stories, and the way how stories influence people, and the other way around. I'd say that really helps in gaining perspective on different people and to highlight the histories or the stories of those who haven't been highlighted before.

Many students who would not have chosen to take humanities courses without a requirement to do so find that studying the humanities is both valuable and enjoyable, and take more courses in this domain. This gives them a richer understanding of social issues than they would have otherwise had:

> A lot of people can come here, as well, . . . already knowing . . . that they're going to do pre-med, for example, and they're going to take a humanities course just for the sake of it. But through experience, I've known a lot of people who have done that and have been like, "Wow. I really enjoyed that as well." Then they go on to do a minor in something which is along those lines as well.

In the European context, liberal education is often associated with freedom of choice in the curriculum. While this is an important aspect of most LAS programmes, it would be a mistake to overlook the importance of the general education component. It is general education that exposes all students to academic work on social issues, giving them a better understanding of such matters but also awakening an interest in current affairs and a desire to keep abreast of them. General education equips them with the knowledge they will need to participate in democratic conversations about society's problems and to make informed choices in the voting booth. This is what it means to be a free citizen in a democratic society, someone who is in a position to make a valuable contribution to the governance of their communities:

> We have to have a wide sense of what being a person today means. [Be] a person [who knows] how our society is developing. If we really contrast these three things, the sciences, the humanities, and social sciences, if we get a little bit of everything, I think we have the skills that are needed to become a free person, to think critically, and to think freely. That relates very strongly to becoming a good citizen in a democratic society because thinking freely is what a democratic society means, I think.

## Notes

1 Plato, *Republic*, book 8.
2 Eva Brann, "A Manifesto for Liberal Education," *The Imaginative Conservative*, 2015, accessed February 22, 2022. https://theimaginativeconservative.org/2022/02/manifestoliberal-education-eva-brann.html.

## Reference

Brann, Eva. "A Manifesto for Liberal Education." *The Imaginative Conservative*, 2015. Accessed February 18, 2022. https://theimaginativeconservative.org/2022/02/manifesto-liberal-education-eva-brann.html.

# 10 The Sense of Democracy and Academic Community

*Having a campus community teaches you that there is something beyond yourself. There's a community that we all live in that's beyond yourself. And participating in extra-curricular activities, which I think is a big part of liberal arts and sciences, helps you develop yourself and develops how you behave in a community. Which, then, will be reflected in how you behave in society as a good citizen. I'm not sure if you can call it a good citizen, but you'll be a tolerated citizen, that's what I would say.*

Having the skills and competencies necessary to participate in democratic conversations is one thing. However, a good citizen is not only able to participate in the democratic process but also wants to do so. Democratic rule depends on people's willingness to engage with other citizens and to contribute to society. Citizens must have what one might call a sense of democracy, a public-spirited desire to work for the common good and, most importantly, to adapt their behaviour to the interests of others, accepting decisions that are taken collectively, even if they might not be in their self-interest:

I would say a good citizen is someone who has an idea about the common good of a society, and who is able to define this, and also to take action to further this common good. These are very broad terms. I think it differs, for example, from just thinking about how I can earn as much money as possible. Being able to look at things from a societal perspective, I would say that's necessary for being a good citizen.

The willingness to work for the common good is perhaps the hardest virtue of all to acquire. In many contemporary societies, fewer and fewer people are willing to devote time to the community, accept compromises, or subject their self-interest to the common good. While many people still vote in national elections, that is the extent of their democratic participation.

DOI: 10.4324/9781003336594-10

Furthermore, the tone of much political and social debate indicates that many people see the democratic process more as an adversarial competition for private gain than a shared search for solutions that benefit everyone. As a result, few such solutions are found.

Acquiring a sense of democracy is a difficult matter because it concerns the development of personal values. Perhaps one could instil the proper values directly, with lectures explaining their importance and rewards for those who display them, but that would be indoctrination of a kind that does not befit a democratic society. However, liberal education provides an alternative. LAS students believe that their education helps them develop a sense of democracy. One key factor is the emphasis LAS programmes place on academic community. They value human relationships as a key part of education and promote social interaction among students, both inside and outside the classroom. Students play an active role within the LAS community, organising events, and participating in discussions about their programmes. This makes LAS programmes quite different from more anonymous ones, in which students file in and out of lecture halls, like ships that pass in the night. As a result, LAS students feel part of a mini-society in which they are academic citizens. Studying and living in such a community, they learn to see the value of being a participating citizen, contributing to the common good, and taking the perspectives or interests of others into account. They often grow attached to a way of life that is characterised by community:

> When you get involved in these discussions and when you meet people from all around the world, when you meet people from different back-grounds, I think it sparks in you this want to change the world and this want to contribute to society.

## The Sense of Democracy

Having a sense of democracy is ultimately a matter of being willing to contribute to society. After all, a democratic society is a collective venture for mutual benefit, and this requires citizens to regulate their behaviour so that it contributes to generating mutual advantage. The sense of democracy is the inclination to apply all the other democratic virtues that have been discussed in one's interactions with others. These other virtues concern abilities and knowledge, and so they are instrumental. However, despite possessing these, one might still not be willing to adapt one's behaviour for the sake of the community. The sense of democracy is a dispositional virtue that is about restraining any such temptation. To do so, one should not always seek to press one's own advantage. Rather than being driven by narrow self-interest, those with a sense of democracy seek to improve the community as a whole. Students often discuss this in terms of wanting to make the world a better place:

> You have an effect on the world no matter what you do, or no matter what choice you make. I do hope that the ones who studied liberal arts and sciences also tend to . . . see that that's the way how things work in a way, and then also try and use it, and seek to change the world, not only for change in general, but change for the better. And in a very principled way talk to their children and say, "Okay, well, the way I leave this world is better than when I got into it." And [seek] to change it for the better in the long term.

Of course, this does not mean that having a sense of democracy requires one to always defer to the interests of others. A good citizen does not have to be a saint. However, one must take the effects of one's behaviour on one's fellow citizens into account in deciding what to do. The interest of the community should feature in one's deliberations and carry considerable weight:

> I think in general [a good citizen is] just someone that cares. That cares about things, that is willing to inform themselves and to think about the well-being of the state, the people, the world in general. Yes, I think it's very much someone who cares and has an interest in taking part in those processes.

Moreover, in making these calculations, one should not take the interests of others into account in a strategic way, seeking to optimise one's behaviour in the light of what others are likely to do. Rather, one should be willing to make some sacrifices for the benefit of the community. However, one should not see these as sacrifices, all things considered, because one sees one's self-interest as tied up with the interest of the community. Realising that they are part of a wider society, a citizen with a sense of democracy is:

> someone who is aware of themselves as not just an individual, but as part of a larger body of people. [It's a matter] of being able and willing to make decisions, whether that's in elections, or in joining in protest movements, or things that aren't always just about what necessarily benefits you as an individual but [what] you think will benefit a wider society, however you consider that wider society and whatever you think your priorities are.

## The Sense of Democracy as a Democratic Virtue

If citizens are to engage in democratic conversations, they must have a sense of democracy. If they are only concerned with their own advantage, the conversation becomes an adversarial process, in which different individuals seek to get their way at the expense of others. What should be a shared exploration of society's problems in search of mutually beneficial solutions becomes a zero-sum negotiation for private gain. Individuals who take this approach in their political interactions with others will undermine the democratic character of the conversation, and hence the governance process. In that sense, they are bad citizens, who were characterised by one student as:

> [being] too selfish and being too self-involved, egocentric. That's not a component you would need as a good citizen, I would say. Because citizenship implies that you interact with others, that there's a whole system of individuals that go together and form society. So, if all those individuals are just being extremely selfish, well, that's your rational choice theory for you, obviously. No, I don't think that gives you the outcome that is the greatest good, if that's a phrase that will work.

A lack of concern for the common good undermines democracy because it goes against several of the central arguments for why one would want a democracy in the first place. One such argument is based on the idea that a democratic conversation, drawing on the wisdom of the many, tends to lead to good decisions. However, this argument supposes that all participants are concerned with the common good, as they understand it. If participants are concerned with their self-interest, there is no reason to think that decisions will be made in the interest of the community as a whole. Rather, the outcome will be determined by who is best able to press their advantage, steer the discussion, get their concerns heard, or silence other voices. In short, if the conversation becomes a competition, those who are best able to compete will win. This attitude runs contrary to the spirit of a democratic conversation. For in such a conversation, it is the force of the better argument that should determine the outcome.

Not only does a lack of a sense of democracy threaten to result in worse decisions, it also undermines the legitimacy of those decisions. One of the great advantages of a democratic conversation is that participants can regard the eventual outcome as legitimate. However, this depends on citizens engaging in the process in good faith, i.e., as a shared search for the common good. If participants are simply engaged in a competition, the outcome cannot be regarded as co-created. Those who did not get their way simply did not get their way, but this gives them little reason to commit to the outcome, in the way they would have if the entire community had come together to collectively decide on the best course of action. It is that kind of engagement that is the substance of democratic conversations, and of democracy generally.

The importance of a collective search for the common good is further underlined by the fact that democracy is based on the value of equality. Recall that, in a democratic conversation, citizens regard each other as equally valid sources of claims. Of course, they may be legitimately partial, both toward themselves and their loved ones, but they must also recognise that others are entitled to be similarly partial. They cannot believe that, from a social perspective, they have the right to dictate what should be done or that their self-interest should count for more than that of others. Rather, seeing each other as equals, they must respect each other's perspectives and interests. This they can do by committing to a process that seeks to weigh all those interests and perspectives, to come to solutions that are, all things considered, the best that can be done for the common good. This makes them good faith participants in democratic conversations:

> Being a good citizen takes [caring] for the community and [knowing] . . . the link between you and your surroundings, and you understanding that there's not one person out of many who can say what everyone wants to do. But in a democracy, you have to talk to your neighbour, and you have to engage with the people in your street, and city, and country, and figure out how you can do things best.

## Teaching the Sense of Democracy Through Academic Community

Students in LAS programmes often feel that their education helps them develop a sense of democracy. While they acknowledge that LAS programmes attract students who are already inclined to be concerned with the common good and making society a better place, they nevertheless report that studying in a LAS programme stimulated their desire to be good citizens. Some students found the reason in the content of the curriculum they studied. As discussed in the previous chapter, LAS programmes teach their students about social issues, in part through general education requirements. Learning about pressing issues tends to make one care about them and want to do something about them. Of course, it is entirely possible to learn about social problems, especially those that occur on a global level, without developing a desire to help solve them. If anything, studying intractable issues can make life feel somewhat hopeless. Nevertheless, engaging with such issues and understanding why they are so problematic for a range of people can also inspire a determination to improve matters. Indeed, sometimes it is the feeling of hopelessness that can foster a desire to make the world a better place by being an active participant in the democratic process:

> because we obviously identify a lot of struggles, issues, and problems that are going on, ranging from climate change to human rights issues, economic crises . . . I think a lot of us face that moment in time when you've gathered a lot of information and you just feel a little bit hopeless [about] why the world is not as ideal as we wish it to be, and I think that goes hand in hand with active participation. Once you've had that moment of hopelessness, the very minimum you can do is, for example, vote, and I think in this way, you are much more inclined to participate in the process.

In addition to this, most students argued that the emphasis LAS programmes place on academic community was a key factor in cultivating their democratic sensibilities. Studying in a closely knit community invites conversations about one's ambitions and values. Inspired by those who are committed to contributing to society, students often decide that they, too, wish to do so. Moreover, being in close contact with each other, students observe the effect their behaviour has on others and, through them, on the community as a whole. They see that the quality of their experiences depends on the flourishing of the community and that they can contribute to this. This can result in a willingness to adapt their behaviour for the benefit of the community, which carries over to society at large.

Many LAS programmes pride themselves on being true communities that value human relationships and social contact. They are characterised by dense social networks and frequent interactions among students, as well as with teachers. Students are expected to organise and participate in extra-curricular activities, such as sports, theatre, fine arts, and the like, but also to attend co-curricular events, which complement the formal curriculum, including guest lectures or debates. In this way, students can apply the knowledge they acquire in their classes in a more social context. Interaction is often facilitated by dedicated facilities; many LAS programmes have their own campuses or buildings, and most have their own common rooms or learning spaces. In some programmes, students live on campus, combining studying, living, and socialising in one physical environment. Other programmes create a residential atmosphere by keeping their buildings open until late in the evening. Not only does this make it possible for students to attend extra-and co-curricular events, it also ensures they run into each other frequently and spontaneously between classes or during study sessions.

While this might be typical for higher education in many parts of the world, it is rare in Europe. It makes LAS programmes different from many large-scale programmes where students file in and out of large lecture halls, going to their classes and then going home, rarely interacting with each other or their teachers. Of course, all universities feature extra-curricular and social activities. However, they are typically not offered in the context of particular programmes, but rather at the university level or by separate organisations, such as fraternities, sororities, or other student associations. This means that they do not ensure that the same students who study together also interact outside of class, reducing the density of their social networks.

Interweaving education and social life, especially when combined with student-centred pedagogies, ensures students' education takes place in a true community. This builds a certain sense of trust and intimacy among students that they would not have in a more anonymous context. In such a community, students discuss a range of questions with each other, including questions about their future plans, ambitions, and values. This forces them to reflect on their own answers to these questions:

> But becoming . . . a better person is more than [that], it's also about your values and being able to reflect on the big questions like freedom [or] equality. How to help other people? Do you have a duty to help them or not? Do you want to become vegetarian or not? All those are big questions or questions I hadn't thought about before coming to [the programme]. Now I have thought about them and I know the different perspectives on those questions, and I think that makes me a better person.
>
> Q: How does that happen in the interaction with others?
>
> Yes, not the academic part of [the programme], but the social part, being a community. . . . Community comes [about] because we have one building, a common room, but also because we take different courses, so we're mixed with everybody. . . . That's how you build a community.

In their communal interactions, in which they talk about their future ambitions and values, students often find that they question or change their values. Those who did not enter the programme with the ambition to contribute to the resolution of social issues sometimes change their minds. Being confronted with people who believe social issues to be important can make one reconsider what one wishes to do with one's life:

> I think, when I started the programme, I always said I'm not somebody who wants to make the world a better place. . . . Then I was very surprised about all the others' dreams of creating NGOs, and of going out

and doing something. I always said to myself that's not my aim. I have shifted a little within the course of my studies that now I think, "Well, I want to do something valuable in my life." Still, not that I would go out and try to solve the crisis in the world, but maybe on some small scale.

This kind of change in attitude is often fostered by being part of discussions and observing that others are actively thinking about how they can contribute to society, both now and in the future. When asked how their education had sparked a desire to be more active politically, one student responded:

It was mostly the fact that other people around me were taking these ideas seriously and were willing to listen to whatever it is you had to say, and then I was like, "Oh, I have nothing to say." I was like, "What do I actually think?" [So, you] step back and then you start developing, I guess.

In figuring out what they think, students can thus be inspired by their peers. When some students are highly active and engaged in causes that they believe contribute to society, others may follow suit, either because they are genuinely excited about doing so or out of guilt:

Some people have been an inspiration to me here. The people that I see, the friends that I have who care about environmental issues, or start environmental clubs on campus, or go to certain protests in [town]. Seeing people active around me has made me question why I'm not as active, to be honest.

If their regular interactions with peers help students develop a concern for the common good, so, too, does their organisation of co- and extra-curricular activities. Students typically play a large role in the creating and running of these events. As a result, they come to understand that what is on offer depends on their actions. If students do not take the initiative, nothing happens. However, if they do, they can help to bring about some wonderful, enjoyable, and sometimes enduring things. This teaches them that contributing to the community can have an impact and that this can be quite satisfying:

We're very tight-knit, we're a very small community. When you're given a task or a project, it's really like, "Okay, this is yours." You can make the best of it, or you can just let it be, and let it fall to the ground. I think the more effort and time I put in, the more I can feel like I've shaped that, and I've made it work . . . how I would like it to work, and how [I would like] it [to] work for other people. . . . I was on the social committee, so I started traditions at our college [with] particular events. For example, I'm from Vienna, so there are always big ball gowns and things. We did stuff like that here. Now I'm proud to say that, "Okay, I started that. I made that happen and now it's here, and it's going to be here for a while."[1]

LAS programmes also frequently involve students in conversations about the management of their programmes and the organisation of their communities. Students are encouraged to take up roles on official bodies and to engage in informal conversations with faculty and leadership. Discussions might concern the academic curriculum, but they might also be about how facilities are managed. The idea is to give students a degree of responsibility for their surroundings, with the hope that they will realise that they can shape that environment through coordinated action. This makes them consider what sort of community they desire:

> Being encouraged to take initiative all the time also encourages [you] to ask questions. How can I make myself happier wherever I am? . . . How can I be more involved in society? That first. How can I be happier in this building? Do I want to recycle my trash? Do I want my homework to be graded in this way or in this way? How do I want my assignments? How do I want my teachers [to teach]?

Of course, questions concerning how to shape a diverse academic community need to be decided on collectively. If a student does something that others do not like, they will immediately be made aware of this, and their actions will come to nothing. However, if they work together with others to come up with popular initiatives, they can help improve things for the student community as a whole. Not only will they themselves benefit directly, but they may come to take pleasure and pride in their achievements. Such positive experiences may then translate into a desire to try to have an impact later in life:

> I think people become, as I said before, sensibilitised for the concerns of others. For the concerns of how, and I think this is also within the architecture of the community, in a small community, you see the consequences [of your] actions. You can see that you can make an impact. Also, that people are supportive of this. I think if you socialise in this manner in these crucial years of your Bachelor's, I think that makes you have a certain outlook on political processes.

In this way, academic community can cultivate a sense of democracy. Giving students, as a collective body, the freedom to shape their communities is, in a way, like allowing them to live in something of a mini-society. Indeed, in many ways, an academic community is just a smaller, special kind of democratic community. If it is a pleasant community, many students will find that they enjoy that way of living, and that the societies in which they fare best in a narrow sense are not always the best, all things considered. This may inspire them to continue to contribute to a democratic way of living as they enter the larger society. Of course, some students will not develop such a sense of democracy, either because they do not find the academic community congenial or because it does not instil in them a sense of democracy that regulates their future behaviour. However, many do develop such a sense of democracy, and this shows that placing more emphasis on academic community is a promising way of helping students become good democratic citizens. After all:

> You can save your country or your continent, or even the world, but let's start in your most concrete environment.

## Note

1   Also appears in Teun Dekker, "Generic Skills Development in European Liberal Arts and Sciences Programmes: A Student Perspective," (Forthcoming).

## Reference

Dekker, Teun. "Generic Skills Development in European Liberal Arts and Sciences Programmes: A Student Perspective." (Forthcoming).

# 11  An Agenda for Teaching Civic Virtue in European Universities

Listening to students reflect on their experiences, it is clear that a LAS education teaches them a range of skills and dispositions that are highly valuable for participating in democratic conversations. Hence, the LAS model might serve as inspiration for other programmes. Some of its features can be applied more widely in higher education, and this promises to help more students acquire the civic virtues they will need to be good citizens.

Needless to say, LAS education hardly has all the answers and does not have a monopoly on teaching civic virtue. Not all LAS graduates become good citizens. Some even become authoritarians or develop anti-democratic sympathies. Nor has a causal, empirically verified link been established between LAS education and civic virtue. Moreover, many non-LAS programmes do sterling work in helping their students become good citizens, albeit often by already incorporating some of the features discussed in the previous chapters.

Nevertheless, the LAS model has something valuable to offer higher education. The evocative accounts of students presented here point to educational concepts and innovations that can help reshape European higher education and make it better serve the democratic societies that students will inhabit. Hence, this final chapter will explore how key aspects of LAS education that help students develop important civic virtues can be implemented in more traditional programmes. By considering how programmes in a broad range of contexts might incorporate these features, a practical educational agenda for teaching civic virtue will emerge.

## Democratic Virtues in European Higher Education

It has been said that changing higher education is like changing a graveyard: one should not expect much help from the people inside. This is an overly cynical view. Clearly, it is unlikely that all of higher education will embrace the LAS model anytime soon. It is one thing to allow new programmes, such as LAS programmes, to be created and for them to become

DOI: 10.4324/9781003336594-11

interesting additions to the higher education landscape, but given the social and professional expectations of what university education is and the existing organisation of institutions, a wholesale overhaul of the typical university programme is not to be expected. At the same time, universities are constantly innovating and experimenting, and many teachers are restless in trying to improve the education they offer. Existing university programmes are always adapting in small ways, making incremental changes to their curricula, pedagogies, recruitment processes, and operations. They do so in response to developments in the disciplines they teach and in response to new educational insights and social change. Hence, it is possible to apply features of the LAS model, including the seven features identified in the preceding chapters, in the context of more traditional programmes.

The first feature of LAS education that traditional programmes might draw on is its multidisciplinarity. One might think there is a fundamental conflict between the multidisciplinary curriculum that is typical of LAS education and traditional disciplinary programmes. After all, what makes a law programme a law programme is that it teaches law. This is required to enable its graduates to become lawyers. It may seem impossible to adapt such a programme to include multiple disciplines without fundamentally undermining it. However, the law does not operate in a vacuum; it is a social phenomenon that is closely linked to other such phenomena. It is made through a political process, its effects depend on social forces, and it influences both the economy and the environment. Acquiring a complete understanding of law thus requires at least some understanding of different disciplines. And there is a case to be made for including these disciplines in law programmes as well. Of course, they might play a supporting role in the curriculum, but they can complement the in-depth study of law by providing multidisciplinary breadth. Similar arguments can be made for any discipline. Hence, there is an academic case to be made for adding other disciplines to traditional disciplinary programmes that complements the civic case for doing so.

Multidisciplinary breadth can be achieved in several ways. A curriculum might require students to take a range of courses in other disciplines. This can be done by offering them a series of elective courses, which has the added benefit of giving them more freedom of choice in their curricula, as will be discussed below. Breadth can also be achieved by incorporating different disciplines into existing courses. For example, a course on regulatory law might include concepts from economics relating to how companies respond to new regulations, as well as insights from sociology on how laws affect marginalised groups and consumers. What is important is that students learn how different disciplines look at various issues and realise that each discipline has something to offer in understanding what is going on. As discussed in Chapter 4, it is this insight that contributes to the open-mindedness that is essential for democratic conversations.

Likewise, traditional programmes might adopt more active, student-centred pedagogies. Such programmes could use discussion-based or student-led approaches, in which students are challenged to scrutinise the information and perspectives they are presented with and to formulate their own answers and views on matters. This should be carried through in how students are assessed. Instead of using exams that merely ask students to recall facts, concepts, and theories or apply them to specific cases, programmes could use open forms of assessment that invite students to develop an individual opinion on scientific and social questions. Their perspectives should, of course, be grounded in what they have studied, but they should make this knowledge their own by thinking about it independently.

Student-centred pedagogical formats are not inherently tied to LAS programmes. Any discipline can be taught actively or passively, in more student-centred or teacher-centred ways. There is ample evidence that student-centred formats result in increased knowledge retention and the development of valuable academic skills. However, what is crucial in this context is that these pedagogies can help students develop independence of thought by schooling them into the habit of not taking the information they are presented with for granted but critically assessing it to come to their own conclusions. It is this capacity that will enable them to meaningfully participate in democratic conversations.

One of the ways in which LAS programmes help students develop a sense of self is by inviting them to develop their own narratives through freedom of choice. Understanding what they like, find interesting, and want to do with their lives can give students a sense of identity which they will need to fulfil their role as citizens in democratic societies. Of course, LAS education has the advantage of allowing students to compose their own curricula, and this forces them to exercise freedom of choice in their education in a way that a more disciplinary programme cannot. In disciplinary programmes, the structure is, to some extent, dictated by the nature of the subject studied. However, even in such programmes, it is possible to give students opportunities to author their own education. As has already been noted, allowing space for elective courses in the curriculum gives students the ability to develop a more individualised academic profile. Students can also be given more freedom within courses. They can be allowed to choose which aspects of a particular topic they wish to study, which literature they desire to read, or which issues they want to write about in their assessments. In this way, students are forced to think about what they find interesting and reflect on what this says about them. This reflection can be further stimulated by encouraging students to discuss their options with their peers or by setting assignments in which they must articulate the rationales for the choices they make. Moreover, giving students greater freedom will help them think about what they want to do after they graduate and in this way develop a more deeply held sense of self.

To help students develop a better sense of the other, traditional programmes could put more effort into attracting students from diverse backgrounds, fostering an international classroom. Any programme can seek to recruit and enrol students from a wide range of backgrounds and will benefit from the resulting diversity. But while many programmes in Europe welcome students from other countries, they rarely invest in attracting such students. Often this is because these programmes do not use student-centred pedagogies, in which a variety of perspectives is likely to benefit the educational process. However, the ambition to help students develop a sense of the other requires a much more active approach to ensuring that the student body is diverse. This might mean offering classes in English, doing outreach activities in other countries, offering scholarships, and redesigning admissions procedures.

The diversity sought should not be only international. Rather, universities should seek to enrol students from a wide variety of social, cultural, and economic backgrounds. This can be a tricky matter, as promoting one kind of diversity can often come at the expense of other forms of diversity. For example, offering courses in English might increase international diversity but make programmes less attractive to local students who come from backgrounds in which it is less common to be exposed to this language. Hence, a balance must be found between different kinds of diversity, to ensure that students encounter a wide range of other students in their education.

Traditional programmes might also assess students based on group projects to teach them the art of compromise. Many group projects in LAS programmes occur in the context of disciplinary courses, so it should not be particularly difficult to add group projects to traditional programmes. At the moment, these programmes tend to focus more on individual work, either in the context of exams or papers, based on the assumption that this is the only way to assess students validly and reliably. After all, many issues complicate group projects, such as how to guarantee that all group members actively participate or how to assess the individual contribution of each student. However, if educators actively coach and monitor group work, asking students to reflect on the collaborative process, one can limit free riding and ensure fair grading.

Including some sort of general education into traditional programmes is a productive way of helping students learn about contemporary social challenges, such as by requiring students to take dedicated courses. Indeed, one might create a shared core curriculum for an entire institution, which students from different programmes attend together. This would have the benefit of promoting conversations about social issues across different programmes. Alternatively, one might integrate discussion of current social issues into disciplinary courses to ensure that students learn about these issues in concert with more subject-specific knowledge. This will ensure that they understand the challenges that society faces, the very challenges that are the subject of democratic conversations.

Lastly, traditional programmes could foster a sense of democracy by taking a more relational approach to education and better integrating academic and social life. This would require dedicated facilities, such as common rooms, but also a commitment from the programme to organise co-curricular activities and to allow students to put on extra-curricular events. Educators would also need to solicit student input into the management of the programme and engage in a constant dialogue about the nature of the education offered. If programmes adopt such a relational approach to education, students might learn the value of being a member of a true community and how this enables them to collectively shape their surroundings, which is what democratic conversations are all about.

If traditional programmes take steps to implement these kinds of measures, it will make them more like LAS programmes, thereby enabling their students to develop the civic virtues they will need to participate in democratic conversations. At the same time, these programmes would still be able to maintain their disciplinary identities. In this way, European higher education could help more students become good citizens.

## The Future of Democratic Conversations

European societies face a range of challenges, such as climate change, international security, inequality, and social polarisation. They must ensure that their people's needs are met, whether that be through healthcare, education, or welfare, and they must provide an environment in which their citizens can flourish. These are big challenges. Meeting them will require concerted action over a long period of time, as well as considerable sacrifice. As many critics of democracy have observed, it is not at all obvious whether this system of government is the best way of dealing with the problems societies face. Competent authoritarian regimes have demonstrated the ability to act and realise dramatic improvements in living standards for their populations. Even within Europe, anti-democratic voices that seek to limit freedom of expression, the rights of minorities, or the rule of law have gained traction.

It is thus up to democratic societies to demonstrate that they can rise to the challenges of the times. Whether they can do so depends on how citizens play their role in the democratic process. After all, the best-designed institutions will falter if citizens do not behave as they are supposed to, while even suboptimal institutions will function to some extent if citizens display a high degree of civic virtue. However, the task is not an easy one. Making collective decisions that serve society and are regarded as legitimate requires sustaining democratic conversations amongst citizens who have different perspectives and interests. There is a constant danger of the conversation degenerating into a negotiation or a contest, undermining democracy from the inside. Every citizen must contribute to democratic conversations. Everyone must ask themselves if they are living up to democratic ideals when they engage with fellow citizens and decide how to act politically.

Rousseau once said that democracy is a system that is so perfect that it is suitable only for Gods, not for mere mortals.[1] Democratic governance, as good-willing people seek to realise it every single day, is an attempt to prove him wrong. There is no denying that this is hard. But that does not mean that we should settle for less. Rather, we should equip our children for the task and have faith that they will do better than we did. This is the highest calling of all education, from the humblest kindergarten to the grandest university. Hence, European higher education stands at a crossroads. Universities can either continue to offer narrow, disciplinary programmes that aim to transmit knowledge efficiently and produce employable graduates, pretending this is the extent of their mandate. Or they can once again embrace their historic role of nourishing human beings' capacity for living together. The LAS model of higher education, as it already exists in Europe, can help universities take up this task. The future of our societies, and their own futures as institutions, depend on it.

## Note

1   Jean-Jacques Rousseau, *Of the Social Contract*, book 3, chapter 4.

# Index

Printed in the United States
by Baker & Taylor Publisher Services